WE WERE
HAPPY THERE

First published in 2014
by Londubh Books, 18 Casimir Avenue,
Harold's Cross, Dublin 6w
www.londubh.ie

1 3 5 4 2

Origination by David Parfrey; cover by bluett.
Printed by Gráficas Castuera, Navarra, Spain.

This book is set in the typefaces Optima, Gill Sans and Adobe Garamond Pro.

ISBN: 978-1-907535-31-4

WE WERE HAPPY THERE

A Hundred Years of
St Louis High School Rathmines

Edited by Ita Daly

LONDUBH BOOKS

In memory of Helen Power SSL,
St Louis High School, Rathmines, 1973-89.

CONTENTS

CONTENTS

CONTENTS

Mary Morgan, Principal

FOREWORD

When the Sisters of St Louis moved into Charleville Road in 1913, I wonder if they could have ever imagined that a hundred years later the school they established in such a modest fashion would still be flourishing and such a well-established and integral part of the community.

This book, which dips in and out of the history of the school, giving us glimpses into past decades as well as a sense of the present day is, I believe, a great achievement. The warmth and humour of the contributors, the stories they tell and the teachers and events they remember show us a school that has evolved and changed with the times but has always remained true to the vision of its founders.

I know how much hard work has gone into producing this book and I would like to thank everybody who has contributed to it. I would also like to thank Jo O'Donoghue, Publisher, Londubh Books, and her layout and design team, David and Syd, for producing such a handsome book.

I would like to thank the committee – Betty Foley, Brídín Gilroy, Dympna Cullen and Pauline Slattery – and especially the editor, Ita Daly, who have devoted many hours to this project.

It is a testament to the strength of community in St Louis High School that these former colleagues collaborated again to bring *We Were Happy There* to fruition. Through their dedication, imagination and flair they have given us a book of which we can all be very proud.

Members of the editorial team for We Were Happy There, *from left: Pauline Slattery, Betty Foley, Ita Daly (editor) and Brídín Gilroy. Dympna Cullen was also a member of the team.*
Photo © Robert Allen Photography.

Ita Daly

INTRODUCTION

On Spy Wednesday 1916 a young woman called Máirín Cregan was in her flat in Grove Road, Rathmines, when she took delivery of a number of guns and some ammunition which she was to transport to the Volunteers in Kerry.

At the time, Máirín, a past pupil of St Louis Convent, Carrickmacross, was teaching in St Louis Convent, Rathmines, and on Holy Thursday she set out for Kerry with a violin case full of guns and ammunition.

She was to return to Dublin on Easter Monday but by then everything had changed – Casement had landed on Banna Strand, Dublin was in the throes of the Rising and the trains weren't running.

When she did get back to Dublin and returned to her work she found that she had been, as she put it: 'dismissed from my teaching post in St Louis Convent, Rathmines. Some of the parents were calling to the Reverend Mother, protesting about their children being taught by a "friend of these rebels" and who herself was strongly suspected of being mixed up in "this rebellion".'

I love this story because it illustrates so clearly how St Louis High School has changed over the years. It went from being a bastion of the establishment, whose purpose was to educate the daughters of the emerging Catholic middle class, to the thriving, inclusive school it is today, embracing change along the way – from Donogh O'Malley's free secondary education to being one of the first schools in Ireland to introduce transition year.

It has been a delight to edit this centenary book. It has brought me into contact with many interesting people and has made me realise how important St Louis High School has been in my life. I met generosity everywhere I went and I would like to thank all the contributors very much for taking the time to lay aside their busy lives to write something for the book. And that something was always interesting, often intriguing, sometimes surprising.

I would like to thank the Principal of St Louis High School, Mary Morgan, for her support and for the many cups of tea that sustained us as we worked on the project. Clíona McDonough was a tremendous help to me, as was Lily O'Donovan. I would also like to thank Miriam Sadlier and her colleagues in the office, who were so patient and helpful throughout.

To the other members of the committee – Dympna Cullen, Brídín Gilroy, Betty Foley and Pauline Slattery – supportive, hard-working and full of ideas, I owe a special debt of thanks. I think it is a lovely book and that is due to Jo O'Donoghue and her design team at Londubh Books.

While we were in the course of preparing this centenary book and in the midst of the school's centenary celebrations, the tragic death of Sister Helen Power occurred. I thought about asking someone to write about Helen but decided that the death was too recent and emotions too raw.

Instead, this book is dedicated to her memory – dear friend, colleague and inspired teacher.

Pauline Slattery

CHARLEVILLE HOUSE

Pauline Slattery recounts the history of Charleville House, Rathmines, which came to embody the educational ethos of the Sisters of St Louis in Dublin.

On 19 November 1912, with the sanction of Archbishop Walsh, Fr Fricker PP, Rathmines, extended an invitation to the superioress of St Louis Convent, Monaghan, to open a secondary day school in Rathmines. On 1 September 1913 St Louis Rathmines opened its doors to students in Charleville House, 27 Charleville Road. In the prospectus, the school was described as a high-class secondary day school, a private school, fee-paying, catering for girls from seven to eighteen, with a kindergarten for children under seven, both boys and girls. The curriculum reflects the educational emphasis for young ladies at that time. Specific reference is made to deportment, manners, self-control, order and neatness, so that the pupils may become not only accomplished but helpful and intelligent in all the duties of woman's sphere. There were ninety pupils on the rolls the first year of the school's existence and in 1914 it is recorded that fourteen students sat the intermediate examination.

At first many of the rooms in the convent were used as classrooms. Over time, as finances allowed, various improvements were carried out. Electric light was first made available in October 1921 and created a wonderful impression all around in the school.

In the early days the Sisters spent their summers acquiring qualifications for the various subjects they taught in the school, as nuns did not yet attend university. It was 1924 when the first two Sisters from Rathmines started in UCD as undergraduates. Three years later these Sisters won scholarships in their degrees.

The Dublin house, Charleville, became a port of call for Sisters from everywhere. There were as yet no nuns' hostels in the city. The school developed greatly and in 1925 three pupils won university scholarships. The following November shrubs were planted in front of the convent. The large field in front of the house was fenced off, in part to graze a cow to provide milk for the Sisters.

In 1929, the Sisters bought Sacred Heart House (8 Grosvenor Road) and in 1942 Wakefield (7 Grosvenor Road). By this time the number of students had reached two hundred. The school vacated the gym in September 1942 and work began to adapt it as a chapel. The marble altar was sent from the old chapel in Monaghan as well as stained glass for the windows. The altar stone came from Gardiner Street convent. The stations of the cross were erected in the chapel in February 1944.

By 1950 the number of students had risen to two hundred and fifty and twelve new classrooms were added. A new convent chapel was opened in 1965 and the gym was also built around this time.

The introduction of free secondary education in 1967 brought sweeping changes to St Louis as a new wave of enthusiasm and idealism gripped education in Ireland. The school expanded rapidly at this time and the Department of Education gave the Sisters a grant to provide accommodation for seven hundred pupils.

After a number of setbacks the official opening of the new wing took place in 1982. Numbers peaked in the mid 1990s and today average six hundred. In 2013, a hundred years after its foundation, St Louis continues as strong as ever: a vibrant progressive school that is diverse in its student population and comprehensive in its curriculum.

* * *

Charleville House, 27 Charleville Road, Rathmines, was designed in 1859 by James Rawson Carroll. Carroll designed several churches and other public buildings and in the course of his distinguished architectural career also built up a considerable country-house practice. In 1875 Carroll acted as assessor in selecting the design for the Church of Ireland glebe house in Rathmines and in 1861 he exhibited architectural designs and models at the Royal Dublin Society's Exhibition of the Fine Arts. He was one of the architects who represented Ireland at the general conference of architects of the Royal Institute of British

The convent and (left) the 1950 wing, designed by T.J. Cullen & Co.

Architects in London in June 1876 and again in June 1878.

According to his obituary in *The Irish Builder*, Carroll was a 'kindly, upright, courteous gentleman' whose 'clients were in a real sense his friends, no trouble was too great for him to take; indeed his attention to detail was extraordinary and therein lay the secret of much of his success.'

Sir John Gray purchased Charleville House on 16 June 1857. A medical doctor with wide-ranging interests, Gray was a Protestant nationalist who had supported Daniel O'Connell's Repeal Association. In 1850 he became sole owner of the leading nationalist newspaper, *The Freeman's Journal*. Elected to Dublin City Council in 1852, he promoted the Vartry water supply scheme against strong opposition and was knighted for this service to the people of Dublin. The first of the statues erected in O'Connell Street (then Sackville Street) in 1879 was of Sir John Gray. A bust by Thomas Farrell, symbolising Gray's social and scientific interests, adorns his grave in Glasnevin.

1913

A. M. ✠ D. G.

Convent of St. Louis,
CHARLEVILLE HOUSE, RATHMINES.

With the sanction of HIS GRACE THE ARCHBISHOP and at the invitation of the VEN. ARCHDEACON FRICKER, P.P., Rathmines, the Sisters of St. Louis have opened a high-class

SECONDARY DAY SCHOOL
 AT THE ABOVE CONVENT.

THE Course of Education includes Religious Instruction; Irish, English, Latin, French, German and Italian Languages; Mathematics, Practical and Experimental Science (Physics, Chemistry, Physiology and Hygiene, Domestic Economy) Commercial Course; Instrumental Music, Singing, Elocution, Drawing, Painting, Dancing, and Hygienic Exercises,

The first aim of the Sisters is to give their Pupils a sound Religious training. Their deportment and manners are carefully attended to; no efforts are spared to enable them to acquire habits of self-control, order, and neatness, so that they may become not only accomplished, but helpful and intelligent in all the duties of woman's sphere.

The School has been fitted with all modern appliances conducive to health, comfort, and progress.

The Session or School year (10 months) consists of two terms, each five months.

FIRST TERM BEGINS ON 1st SEPTEMBER.

SECOND TERM BEGINS ON 1st FEBRUARY.

Fees are to be paid strictly in advance.

For particulars apply to
THE SUPERIORESS.

On 28 January 1890 the trustees of Sir John Gray's estate passed the deeds of Charleville House on to the Loreto Sisters, who had a school in Kenilworth Square. The school building was burned and in 1889 the Sisters took up residence in Charleville. They left it in July 1912 and on 22 July of that year the property passed to a wealthy businessman, William McCabe, who sold it a year later to the St Louis Sisters.

According to conservation architect David Slattery, the name 'Charleville House' is slightly misleading, as Charleville seems originally to have comprised a pair of interconnecting houses. As it now stands the original 19th-century residence is clearly identifiable from the later developments that took place as St Louis High School grew.

Charleville stands two storeys over a semi-basement. The main façade is four-bayed and bookended with recessed entrance bays, with entrance porches and arched windows overhead. The general detail is mid-Victorian and features brick walls with granite quoins and cornices. The entrance steps are also in cut granite. Earlier illustrations of Charleville show original Georgian sash windows and a glazed conservatory on the southern porch. The house has well-proportioned reception rooms with original decorative features.

Charleville appropriately embodies the history of the St Louis Sisters in Rathmines. It commands its setting within its original grounds and despite the way in which the school developed in close proximity it retains its dignity and integrity.

Left: Prospectus for Convent of St Louis Secondary Day School, 1913.

Eilís Ní Thiarnaigh SSL giving her presentation in Rathmines library.

Eilís Ní Thiarnaigh SSL

THE COMING OF THE SISTERS OF ST LOUIS

As part of the centenary celebrations, on 22 October 2013 Éilís Ní Thiarnaigh SSL gave a presentation to a large, appreciative audience in Rathmines library about the coming of the Sisters of St Louis to Rathmines a hundred years ago. This is a synopsis of her talk.

On 13 November 1912 Mother Antonia Farrell, Mother Superior of the St Louis Convent in Monaghan, received a very unexpected letter. It came from the parish priest of Rathmines, a town which was then outside the boundaries of Dublin city, and invited her to open a convent and school in the parish.

To have a house in the vicinity of Dublin was something the Sisters of St Louis hoped for when they first came to Ireland but it had not happened until now – so Mother Antonia must have been pleased. On the other hand, as she was about to open the congregation's first house in England in the New Year, she was concerned about the financial and personnel outlay of another foundation following so soon. She also wondered why it was that the Loreto Sisters, who had had a school in Rathmines for several years, had suddenly left.

After some investigation, she discovered that it was very difficult for a Catholic school to make ends meet as the population of the area was mainly Protestant. She put her trust in God, however, as she said in her reply to Archdeacon

Fricker: 'If God wills the work for our country, He will remove that obstacle as He has other obstacles in the past.' She consulted her local bishop, Dr McKenna, and made the decision to accept the offer to go to Rathmines. By the summer of 1913 she had bought a house and approximately three-and-a-half acres of land in the area.

Everything was going smoothly, except that Archdeacon Fricker had only the verbal agreement of the Archbishop of Dublin, Dr William Walsh, and he needed the archbishop's written approval before he could announce his new scheme to the people of Rathmines parish. Mother Antonia was naturally worried, as there was much to be done to get the convent and school ready for opening in September. She therefore wrote a carefully-worded, diplomatic letter to Dr Walsh, thanking him for giving the Sisters of St Louis the opportunity to work in his diocese.

The archbishop seems to have been quite uneasy about this new venture, one that involved bringing Sisters in from another diocese. He wrote to Archdeacon Fricker, 'How do we get them out if they are not satisfactory?' His solution was that the Sisters of St Louis would be on a probationary period of five years and would have to leave then if he was not satisfied with them.

Mother Antonia had no choice but to accept this and other peculiar conditions the archbishop imposed, e.g. that the Sisters would not attend any lectures in the university, or visit the poor or the sick in the area. She did, however, negotiate for one thing that was important to her, that this new foundation would continue its connection with the motherhouse in Monaghan. Rathmines was, in fact, the first house in Ireland to be able to keep this connection and not come wholly under the control of the local bishop.

So at last the way was clear for the Sisters to prepare the convent and school for 1 September 1913. The school opened under the guidance of its first principal, Sr Raphael Nugent, with just thirty-six pupils on the first day. Good reports must have circulated around the area in the next few days, as eighty pupils turned up in the second week. Thus began a successful first year of St Louis High School, a school that this year, 2013, is celebrating its centenary.

The image contains the text: "THE EMPLOYERS VICTORY IS SHORT LIVED. IN JUNE 1914 LARKIN IS ELECTED PRESIDENT OF THE IRISH TRADE UNION CONGRESS AND WITHIN A FEW SHORT YEARS THE MEMBERSHIP OF THE ITGWU HAS SWELLED TO 120,000. IN THE WORDS OF SEAN O'CASEY "A TINY SPECK OF FLAME HAD BECOME A PILLAR OF FIRE""

2013 was a year of centenaries and twenty St Louis students participated
in the 1913 Lockout Tapestry project, joining students from Larkin Community College
and Mater Dei Primary School, Basin Lane, in creating the final panel
– the torch of hope carried into the future.
Tapestry designed by Cathy Henderson and Robert Ballagh.
Photo by kind permission of the Lockout Tapestry Committee.

Angela Bourke

WITH MISS INGRAM

Frances Ingram was a St Louis institution for decades but Angela Bourke saw the sweet, sociable child behind the middle-aged teacher when she visited her in her home.

'I'm pulling and dragging,' Miss Ingram would say, when the girls down the back chatted too loudly for her to continue. 'Pulling and dragging, trying to teach you Latin!'

We weren't afraid of Miss Ingram – she had no cruelty or sarcasm – but she may have been afraid of us. Her cheeks often wobbled and grew red as a class wore on and all of us could imitate her constant gesture with forefinger and thumb, wiping away the lipstick that collected at the corners of her mouth, leaving her lips bare. She was turning sixty: a little younger than we are now. Small and round, with short, smooth, grey-brown hair that was parted at the side and curled around the edges, she wore twin sets – fine knitted jumpers under matching cardigans in dusty pink or mossy green, buttoned tightly across her stomach, with straight tweed skirts

that came below her knees. Her glasses were on a chain around her neck; her lace-up shoes were flat and brown; her stockings tan nylon, like ours, but thicker, and she wore cotton knickers in pink or blue, with elasticated hems that clasped her legs a little above the knee.

The teacher's desk in our Leaving Certificate classroom stood on a platform and instead of what office-supply shops call a 'modesty panel', it had legs. When Miss Ingram sat down, as she did at the beginning of every class, she stayed seated, her feet barely touching the floor. For the next forty-five minutes, as she talked and gestured, her skirt would ride up around her solid middle until the knickers appeared, consoling us in the front rows for the painful repetitions of Caesar's *Gallic Wars*. We liked style and wit in teachers but by the time we

22

LE COUCHER DU SOLEIL

Comme je me promène, par un beau soir de l'Automne, le long d'une route dans les montagnes de Dublin, les heures, les moments se passent et moi, je regarde le coucher du soleil. C'est devant moi, un spectacle si splendide, que je m'y perds dans la contemplation.

Au-dessus de l'horizon dans l'azur du ciel, des petits nuages floconneux, couronnés de l'or, s'entassent en haut, et le grand soleil se couche tout lentement. Quelques instants après, il devient rouge, et le ciel même est si enflammé qu'on pourrait croire qu'il brûle. De plus en plus il se couche, et puis il partit, mais non sans avoir fait un autre geste dramatique, il perce entre les nuages, en complétant cette vision de splendeur.

Est-il rien de plus agréable que de regarder d'en haut le spectacle qui se déroule au devant des yeux? comme " je promène au hasard mes regards sur la plaine." Derrière moi, les grandes montagnes, comme des sentinelles, teut baignées dans la lumière vive et rouge du soleil, qui leur fait adieux. Au loin, à droite, le havre de Dun Laoghaire, mais si petit, comme celui d'un tableau. Au devant à-peine peut-on voir les monuments les plus grands de la cité, et peu à peu tout se couvre d'une brume bleue.

Quel calme et quelle sérénité!

A cet instant, sur la branche d'un vieil arbre, j'aperçois tout tremblant, un petit oiseau, qui chante sa mélancolique chanson.

Déjà c'étaient formés autour des collines á l'est, des nuages noirs. Quand on voit ces montagnes-ci, devenues tout á coup silencieuses, an moment où, tout doucement, dans ce coin écarté du monde, la nuit déscend, et répand sur la terre, pour quelques heures, son ombre et son calme, on sait qu'en ce moment de silence, la nature nous parle.

Jugez de quel émotion on peut comprendre l'esprit des poètes, qui personnifient l'esprit même de la nature, et qui en ont si bien compris les beautés; quand on contemple ce tableau-ci, et quand on entend la musique de la nature; le murmure de l'eau qui coule, les feuilles qui tremblent dans le vent, ont une musique étrange et fascinante, qui charme celui qui veut l'écouter et l'entendre. Mais tant de choses sont communes à ceux qui la comprennent et l'aiment.

Peu à peu, du silence un bruit se lève, distinct à peine, mais bientôt an sommet d'une colline tout près de moi, un homme vient. Il marche tout lentement chez lui, à une petite chaumière rustique, devant laquelle, à la porte, sa femme l'attend. Elle sourit comme il s'approche d'elle, ils causent à voix basse, puis ils entrent dans la chaumière, et tout est déserte encore et presque noir.

F. INGRAM.

knew her, Miss Ingram had neither and the Latin curriculum didn't help. She had been to Rome, though, and it wasn't hard to distract her by asking about the buildings of the ancient city. Beaming as she recalled them, she would describe their size and beauty and magnificent engineering and the sunshine in which they stood. Her most detailed account was of the Cloaca Maxima, whose great size she indicated by waving her arms above her head. It was the main sewer for the city of Rome but she gave no sign of noticing the choked laughter that greeted her answer to a question about its function and showed only approval in the months that followed, whenever someone innocently asked, 'Please, Miss Ingram, tell us about the Cloaca Maxima.'

Miss Ingram was a past pupil, her happy, trusting smile discernible among the old school photographs downstairs, above a gym-slip like our own and a camogie stick. Apart from infancy and university, she had spent her life at St Louis; she still lived in her childhood home, on Leinster Road West, and her greeting for any wine-coloured uniform she met in the street was dignified but warm. She had nothing to hide: even the nickname we knew her by was innocent: Fanny, for Frances.

When Miss Ingram caught bronchitis in our fifth year and was out of school for weeks, two of us who lived not far away volunteered or were commandeered to visit her on our way home. We were hugely curious about our teachers' private lives. Domesticity in Dublin 6 remained heavily veiled behind lace curtains and closed doors; we knew our own homes and a few others and that was all; and for all our snorting at sensible underwear and the architecture of ancient Rome, we were Louis girls, with a leaning towards good deeds and a keen interest in becoming 'mature', so it was a heady thing to open the cast-iron gate and walk up the path to Miss Ingram's front door.

The 1911 census records for 4 Le Bas Terrace, Rathmines, show that Frances Margaret Ingram was two in April of that year. Her English-born father, Edward Addison Ingram, aged thirty-five, was a post office clerk; her mother, Elizabeth Mary Stanislaus Ingram, born in County Wicklow, was thirty-one and they were five years married. Their eldest child, Frederick, was four, and the youngest, Edward, eight months old. He must be the Eddie Ingram, born in Dublin on 14 August 1910, who played cricket for Ireland forty-eight times between 1928 and 1955, and captained the team eight times. Described by *Wisden Cricketers' Almanack* as 'a great character of Pickwickian girth', he also gained a cap for Middlesex and died in England in 1973.

We waited some time at the door but didn't have time to be embarrassed when it opened to reveal Miss Ingram in a belted Foxford dressing-gown and slippers, with her hair in a net and her nose red, coughing. When she asked us to wait, we stood solemnly in the long, wide hall as she made her way back up the stairs and prepared to receive us.

Hoarse calls drew us up to the half-landing on the return, with a glimpse of an old-fashioned bathroom and a bedroom beyond, then up a short flight to the landing and the half-open door of the front bedroom. It was a big room, the full width of the house, with a fireplace at the far end and two tall windows. Heavy furniture that must have belonged to Miss Ingram's parents left plenty of empty floor but she beckoned us to chairs beside the double bed, where she sat facing the windows, straight-backed in her long-sleeved nightdress, with pillows at her back and her hands on the candlewick bedspread, no book in sight.

I don't know if we made a hot drink or did anything useful for her before we tiptoed down the stairs and pulled the hall door after us but talking to her was surprisingly easy. The candlewick bedspread peaked where her toes stuck up beneath it but that was less than halfway down and the rest of the bed was entirely undisturbed. She must have smoothed it just before we came upstairs but what I still see is a sweet and sociable little girl, proud to be spending the day in her parents' bed as a treat, because she had a bad cough.

Frances Ingram.

Betty Ann Norton

MEMORIES OF ST LOUIS 1945-52

Betty Ann Norton remembers performances and chastisements and sees in the corridors 'the ghosts of girls in wine gym slips with three pleats back and front'.

I went to school on the Number 15 tram, which had an open front section on the upper deck that woke me up. The tram went up Rathmines Road with the odd lurch. Class was in Wakefield, Grosvenor Road (now Number 7, I believe); we were seated on armchairs in front of a live fire in an emerald-green stove. I wonder if it's still there.

We later had classes in the laboratory, which was in the main house – the large room situated closest to the main foyer of the present school (which in the 1940s had not yet been built). The lab had a skeleton in a cupboard (literally) and in front of the open cupboard I regaled the class with 'Kitty the Hare' ghost stories filched from *Our Boys* magazine. Other 'things to do'

included helping Sr Gemma with the 'babies' in St Louis Hall (long since demolished).

My happiest memory of St Louis Hall was parading around in a crêpe paper dress and hat in turquoise and maroon (the school colours) as 'the New Look in St Louis'. It was 1950 and Dior had just designed the New Look. I won first prize.

Fellow students who were part of this happy group included Emily Lynch, Anne Gaskin, Toni Donoghue, Valerie Hart, Alice Curtis and Nuala Nelson. We wore velour hats with a brim, white gloves on outings, black tights (stockings I guess) and did not eat in the street.

Betty Ann Norton playing the trumpet at a performance of Pinocchio, *2007.*

One particular memory still nags. One sunny day (during school holidays) Valerie Hart (later Valerie McGovern and an RTÉ presenter) and I were in Rathmines library selecting our books. Armed with the books, we decided to walk up to the school for a stroll around the field, as we then called it. We were dressed in new white blouses, navy slacks and school blazers (wine piped with turquoise braid). We were full of ourselves but we were soon to be deflated. As we passed the grotto we were pounced on by Sr Anselm, who ordered us home to take off our brothers' trousers. 'How dare you wear trousers – and with the school blazer. You are a disgrace to the school!' We were totally crushed and slunk out the school gates that we had entered so blithely. The same Sr Anselm taught us home economics in secondary school and I could never thread the sewing machine to her satisfaction.

I have many happier memories of secondary school: Mary Cahill's soaring voice in *The Student Prince*, Hazel Yeoman's showstopper, 'Prune Brandy', my crinoline in the role of the Archduchess Maria Victoria, which on the instructions of the late Maureen Bourke of Bourke's Costumers in Dame Street, 'must have a dressing room to itself.' It and I were installed in the small teachers' room. There was no comment from Miss Stuart (who praised me in English class and ignored me in maths class, which I thought was very perceptive of her) or from Miss Hayes (who taught science and geography) but Miss Ingram complained that 'the teachers have nowhere to powder their noses'.

I also have happy memories of Sr Frances Teresa, our headmistress and English teacher, who read *Julius Caesar* to us, the elegant Sr Miriam who recited Marvell so mellifluously, the diminutive Sr Trea scolding us for sucking our art brushes and tall Sr Clothilde waving her baton and imploring us not to 'scoop' as we sang.

When the 'shoebox' headdresses vanished, nuns who had been tall and commanding became a mere five foot nothing.

Our head girl was the wonderful Eilís Mullan, who loved working out geometry theorems herself and checking her answer in the textbook, while the rest of us tried to learn them by rote. Eilís and I became great friends and her early death was a great sadness. Margaret Smith was the genius at art and Emily Lynch scored at camogie, which I avoided like the plague when a red-headed Kerry girl joined the team. She was christened 'Tin Opener' by the witty Emily.

I see the ghosts of girls in wine gym slips with three pleats back and front bobbing and ducking down corridors as they hold doors for teachers and curtsy to all the Sisters they meet: 'Go mbeannaí Dia dhuit.' It took a long time to traverse a corridor in those days.

And more, much more, than in my verse can sit,
Your own glass shows you when you look in it.
WILLIAM SHAKESPEARE, 'SONNET 103'

Ita Daly

LYLA KENNEDY: A ST LOUIS GIRL

Ita Daly meets a past pupil who epitomises what it means to be a 'St Louis girl'.

I f anyone can be called a St Louis girl surely it must be Lyla Kennedy. Lyla Gogan, as she was then, started school in high babies in 1932 and did her Leaving Certificate in St Louis High School in 1944. When she married and had her own family, of course they went to St Louis – the boys to the babies and her two daughters, Eilís and Helen, right through the school system up until Leaving Certificate. Not content with this connection, Lyla was back working in the school as bursar during Sr Kathleen O'Sullivan's reign.

When I met Lyla in her house in Knocklyon she was full of memories of her schooldays. She was a local girl, her family having lived on Maxwell Road. Her aunts before her had gone to the same school building but in those days it was run by the Loreto nuns. Most of the girls were local, coming from Rathmines and Rathgar, with the odd one making the journey from the newer suburb of Terenure.

Lyla entered the high school in 1939. It was a tiny school, encompassed by what is now the concert hall. There were three lay teachers – Miss Ingram, Miss Hayes and Miss Stuart – all three of whom were still going strong when I arrived in 1956. They were known to Lyla and her friends as 'the Wishing Nuts' and their staffroom (known as the teachers' room) was the doorway of Sacred Heart House!

'A doorway?' I asked.

Lyla with Sr Helena, 1947.

'Like a porch but the glass panels were coloured and it was always dark in there. Before that there was only what we girls called a hut. And that was where Miss Stuart continued to smoke.'

When Lyla first went to school, lunch was eaten on the premises, usually a sandwich. After school her mother would have a hot dinner waiting for her. But all that was to change during the war when the lunchtime break was extended so that the girls could go home to a hot meal in the middle of the day. The gas was on at that time, with fathers arriving home too. There was strict rationing of gas with the 'glimmer man' doing the rounds to see that it was enforced.

When talking to Lyla, I got the impression that the high school was somewhere she was happy and content.

'I think we all were – it offered so much.'

As I have said, the school was small with only one class in each year. In Lyla's Leaving Certificate class in 1944 there were just sixteen girls.

'What subjects did you study for the Leaving?'

'Irish, English, History, Geography and Physiology.'

'And extracurricular activities?'

'Ah.' Her face lit up.

The high school was a top camogie school in those days and Lyla was on the team that won the Dublin County Championship and the Dublin League. The championship was played in Croke Park and the league in the Phoenix Park. On both occasions the winning team marched down the middle of the street to the Monument Creamery, where victory food was dispensed. Lyla has two medals for camogie and obviously loved the game. As I looked across at her, straight and slim, I could imagine her wielding a camogie stick even today.

The school always had a strong musical tradition. Musicals and plays were performed in Lyla's day and she enjoyed taking part in them. In 1940 she had a starring role in *The Bohemian Girl*. There was also a school orchestra and Lyla played the cello, bringing it home from school on her bike.

She remembers the old habit the nuns wore, with the square box-like headgear. She and her friends had fun guessing what colour the nuns' hair might be – their only chance to find out was when a nun might scratch her head. She also did messages for the nuns, running up and down to McManus's chemists and exchanging unwanted medicines for soap.

When she left school she continued to have close ties with it through the past pupils' union and the past pupils' musical society and she was one of the people who started the parents' union. In 1974 she came to work in the office as the school bursar. Sr Kathleen O'Sullivan was principal and I remember what a formidable team they made.

Were the girls different from her day?

'Much more open.'

After our interview, Lyla graciously asked me if I would like a cup of tea. As she brought in a tray set with china and laden with goodies, I thought to myself: she is still every inch a St Louis girl.

Right: Lyla with John Conroy and Pat Russell at the first St Louis High School drama festival, December 1971.

Above: The brand-new Carnegie Library, 1913.
Below: Rathmines Road looking south, showing tram lines.
Images reproduced courtesy of the National Library of Ireland.

Iseult Deane and Sharon Muldoon

RATHMINES IN 1913

Iseult Deane and Sharon Muldoon look back at the 'affluent suburb'
of south Dublin that was largely Protestant, Unionist and royalist (except
for the servants) when the Sisters of St Louis came to Charleville House in 1913.

In 1913 Rathmines was an affluent suburb of Dublin. The name 'Rathmines' derives from the de Meones family, who settled on these lands in 1280. By the early 1900s the centre of the city was becoming overcrowded and polluted and the prosperous middle classes started to move out to the new suburbs of Rathmines, Monkstown, Donnybrook and Sandymount on the south side and Clontarf on the north. The large Georgian houses they left behind often became tenement buildings.

From the 1850s, transport from Rathmines to the city centre was by horse-drawn omnibus. In 1871, work commenced on the Dublin tram system on Rathmines Road, just before the Portobello Bridge, and a horse-drawn tram service was in place the following year. By 1913 interest was growing in a newer form of transport – the motor car. The Ford Motor Company sold six hundred cars in Ireland in 1913 and some of these would certainly have been bought by wealthy people in Rathmines.

The Temple family owned the area of Rathmines in the early part of the 19th century and their names are still associated with it. Henry John Temple, later Lord Palmerston, became British Prime Minister in 1855 and his family is responsible for much of the development of Rathmines. This can be seen in placenames such as Palmerston, Grosvenor, Richmond and

Temple. In the mid-19th century there was a building boom in Rathmines. Wide roads, such as Palmerston Road, Temple Road and Rathgar Road, were built. In 1913 the vast majority of the residents of Rathmines were staunch supporters of the monarchy and considered themselves Anglo-Irish. They lived in large houses with basements that allowed for a live-in servant. Kitchens occupied the basements of the houses.

Writer Sydney Gifford (1889-1974), who was born in 8, Temple Villas, describes the Rathmines of her upbringing: 'Our family home in Dublin was on the south side, in what was called a "good residential district", which meant, in those days, a stronghold of British imperialism. The people who surrounded us were lifelike but inanimate models of distinguished English people. It was a deadly atmosphere, in which any originality of thought or independence of action was regarded as eccentricity or lawlessness. You have guessed it! This was Rathmines.'

She also describes the strange artificial English accent adopted by the residents of the suburb as the 'Rathmines drawl'. The playwright Sean O'Casey even used the idea of the very proper and posh 'Lady from Rathmines' getting lost in the city centre during the 1916 Rising for comic effect in *The Plough and The Stars*.

One of the most prominent buildings in Rathmines at the time was the town hall. As well as being used for the business of local government, it was a centre for social events in the early 20th century. When Edward VII visited Rathmines town hall in 1911 it was a great occasion for the population of the township. Anything to do with the monarchy or the king's representative (the viceroy) was a big social event. The doings of the viceroy, Lord Aberdeen, and his wife were reported in detail in all the fashionable papers.

The king's birthday was celebrated each year in Rathmines. The celebrations involved a band marching up Palmerston Road, with Union Jacks hanging from some of the houses. When it arrived at Palmerston Park, it played a number of tunes in the king's honour. This continued until 1920.

By 1913 Rathmines was no longer entirely the preserve of the Protestant upper-middle classes. Some wealthy Catholic families owned houses in the area, one of the most prosperous being the Plunketts. Pat Plunkett, grandfather of Joseph Mary Plunkett (signatory of the 1916 Proclamation), built houses on Palmerston Road and Cowper Road. He lived in 14 Palmerston Road until his death at the age of a hundred and one. His house had extensive grounds and included a tennis court and paddocks, where the family kept their carriage and horses.

Joseph Plunkett's maternal grandfather, Patrick Cranny, built many of the houses on Belgrave Road, as well as dwellings in Donnybrook and Ballsbridge.

From the late 19th century a sense of nationalism was developing in Ireland. Poor living and working conditions in the city led to industrial strife that culminated in the Lockout of 1913. Many of the prosperous inhabitants of Rathmines had no desire to embrace nationalism or change the political situation. Living in the suburbs meant that they could isolate themselves from this threat. Cultural change in the form of a Gaelic revival was also taking place. The Gaelic League had more than six hundred branches in the country and the GAA was flourishing and had spread its activities to every parish in Ireland. While all this was going on the Anglo-Irish and the Catholic middle classes in the grander houses were still entertaining at home with afternoon teas, refusing to believe that change was coming.

As living conditions in the city continued to deteriorate, more and more people began looking for a way out. Some took up work as servants to the wealthy, living in the basements of large houses in the suburbs, including Rathmines. During the First World War, with many men gone to fight with the British army, it became harder for families to afford servants. This change affected domestic architecture: houses were now usually built with the kitchen on the same level as the dining room, as much of the cooking was done by the families themselves. With large numbers of houses being built, many middle-class Catholic families moved from the city to Rathmines. In Belgrave Square, for example, 46 per cent of the householders were Roman Catholic.

When Cowper Gardens was developed an *Irish Times* property advertisement gave an outline of the sort of lifestyle you would expect if you moved to Rathmines: 'You could settle in one of these charming villas with the knowledge that a better choice of home in Dublin is impossible, with charming views of the Dublin Mountains and the new golf links and all town advantages. By train or tram you can be in the centre of Dublin in a few minutes.'

Many nationalists who played a pivotal role in the Rising and the War of Independence lived in Rathmines, including Cathal Brugha, Nora Connolly O'Brien (daughter of James Connolly), the Gifford Sisters and Constance Markievicz. The pacifists Hannah and Francis Sheehy-Skeffington also lived there. Other notable residents of Rathmines around 1913 include the artists Jack Butler Yeats and Walter Osborne, writer and artist George Russell and, a little later, Annie M.P. Smithson, the novelist and poet.

In 1913 Rathmines Public Library was officially opened in the building we know today. It had been expanding and changing since 1887. It was funded by a grant from Andrew Carnegie, who donated to the building of museums and libraries in America, Britain and Ireland, including Carnegie Hall in New York. It was designed by the architectural firm of Bachelor and Hicks to match the style of the town hall and clock tower opposite. Along with book-lending services, Rathmines Library provided a newspaper reading room and a lecture hall. The latter was converted into Ireland's first children's library ten years later.

Also in 1913 the Princess Cinema, the first picture palace in Dublin, opened in Rathmines and the library holds its only remaining plaque. The first film shown there was a recording of the 1913 Epsom Derby, during which suffragette Emily Davison ran into the race as a form of protest and was trampled by the king's horse. The cinema's original building was demolished in 1982.

The Rathmines and Rathgar Musical Society was also founded in 1913. The objectives of the society were the study and production of operatic, choral and other high-class musical works and its first production was *The Mikado*. The first chairperson of the society was William Martin Murphy, one of the employers at the centre of the Lockout. Constance Markievicz's husband, Casimir, took part in one of the society's productions in 1914.

In 1824 a plot of land of two-and-a-half acres was purchased from the Earl of Meath as a site for Rathmines Catholic Church, the first to be built in the district. It was consecrated in 1830. A prominent feature is the copper dome. The original dome was destroyed in a fire in 1920 and replaced by the current dome when the church reopened in 1922. It was said that the dome was to be used in St Petersburg but political upheaval in that city in the aftermath of the Russian Revolution caused it to be diverted to Dublin.

Sources: Deirdre O'Kelly, *Four Roads to Dublin* (O'Brien Press, 1996), St Louis High School history department and Sisters of St Louis archive.

St Louis Convent Rathmines camogie team,
winners of Dublin Schools' League and Championship, 1942.

Mary Black

LITTLE DUBLIN SINGER

Celebrated performer Mary Black began her musical career
with Sr Herman in the Little Dublin Singers.

I started in St Louis primary school in 1959. I vividly remember, at the age of four, walking up the steps, along the corridor and into Sr Norbert's class in Room 4. I was the only girl from Charlemont Street who went to St Louis and this made me feel very important and special!

Both my parents had always enjoyed and encouraged music at home so when I was picked for a place in the Little Dublin Singers at the age of seven they were delighted and very proud. The school was renowned for its choir and I always say that my time as a member there has stood to me in my own career in music. It taught me the importance of hard work, it gave me a great understanding of harmony and it instilled in me the confidence to be a leader with my voice. Sr Herman was a tough taskmaster but always managed to get the very best performance from all the girls!

I was very lucky because by the time it came for me to go to secondary school, free education had become available to all children in Ireland. This meant I could stay in St Louis; otherwise I would have had to leave and attend a technical school as my parents would not have been able to afford the fees.

My school years were some of the happiest in my life and I still have great friends from my time there.

Barbara Fleming

MEMORIES OF
SR MIRIAM

Sr Miriam was a gifted teacher of English and History, giving Barbara Fleming a love of the French grand siècle, *the 17th century, with its poets and dramatists.*

It is said that no one forgets a good teacher and after more than fifty years I still cherish happy, vivid memories of Sr Miriam, our history teacher in St Louis High School.

In those far-off days schoolbooks had small, tight print and few, if any, had illustrations. History books tended to be heavy with dates of battles and lists of kings and emperors and gave little or no insight into the social or domestic life of people long ago. Well before the advent of audio-visual aids it was a real challenge to make history living and interesting. For Leaving Certificate I well remember studying *The Ascendancy of France in the Seventeenth Century,* a dense, heavy volume, but Sr Miriam, with her excellent command of English, fired us

with enthusiasm, bringing the book to life with descriptions of scenes in Parisian salons or the opulent court of Versailles. For us teenagers of the dull, grey 1950s, what an exciting, colourful world to which to escape! We shivered as we debated the identity of Alexandre Dumas's man in the iron mask and hugely admired each of the dashing three musketeers. Historical novels helped to fire our imagination. I remember being enthralled by readings from Nancy Mitford's *The Sun King*, with its dazzling portrayal of the king's mistresses. We were fascinated when Sr Miriam told us very matter of factly that this was 'recognised practice' at the time.

Far from the glamour of Versailles, she was also

a great fan of Czar Peter the Great, who sought to modernise Russia, working in the shipyards of Holland and seeking his 'window on the Baltic'. We developed a lasting interest in the early development of Eastern (in the 1950s Communist) Europe, with its vast expanses of land and huge divide between the ruling classes and the common people.

When I went on to study French literature, I was very grateful to Sr Miriam for giving me such knowledge and insight into *le grand siècle*, with its poets and dramatists. A devotee of politics, she gave us our first insights into the workings of the political system – indeed, ours must have been one of the first schools to visit Dáil Éireann. Not until much later did we realise how privileged we were, when we met so many people who had been 'bored' with history and had little interest in their Irish or European heritage.

Many years later, when she retired, Sr Miriam took on the demanding task of looking after the St Louis archives in the community's motherhouse in Monaghan but the job must have been dear to her historian's heart.

But perhaps most past pupils will remember her best as an inspiring teacher of English, who encouraged wider reading when novels were not part of the curriculum. I still recall her beautiful voice as she read Keats's 'Ode to a Nightingale' or dramatic scenes from *Henry IV*. She blazed a trail by introducing students to debating and public speaking. Her highly organised, carefully labelled cupboard on the top corridor contained cuttings on current affairs from *Time* magazine and newspapers like the *Observer*. Again, it was only years later that St Louis past pupils realised how great their debt to our reserved, gifted, enthusiastic teacher, Sr Miriam.

Sr Miriam Commins.

Vincent Kennedy

CUISLE

*Vincent Kennedy celebrates a beautiful chapel of the 1960s,
now the creative and spiritual pulse of St Louis High School.*

This beautiful building, the former convent chapel, was leased to St Louis High School by the Sisters of St Louis from the mid-1990s and named 'Cuisle' ('pulse'). It was officially opened in 2002. Regrettably, the building was no longer needed as a chapel, due to falling numbers in the congregation and in the local community. There were serious problems in relation to the heating system, which was ineffective, and the building was in need of extensive maintenance.

This house of prayer was built 1962-4 and consecrated in 1965. No expense was spared in its construction or ornamentation. The windows on either side of the altar were among the largest in these islands, second only to Clifton Cathedral in Bristol, which was consecrated a decade later.

An observer in the gallery on a sunny morning will witness the extraordinary brilliance and quality of the light and the vibrancy of the colours filtered through the exquisite stained-glass windows designed by David Willis and installed in 1967. The extensive use of rich wood throughout – Parana pine in the high roof and Japanese oak in the stalls and benches – further enriches the warm and welcoming atmosphere of the interior. Geometric shapes are used in the roof and the side windows, especially the triangle, a reminder of the significance of the Holy Trinity in the theology of Christianity.

A haven from noisy classrooms and the school yard, the chapel was a place of contemplation, a house of peace, a space in which to pray, meditate, worry, rejoice and reflect on issues occupying the minds of the Sisters who gathered here several times a day. The dulcet tones of the plainchant harmonies, the unison prayers and the sometimes sombre but normally joyful liturgies that were celebrated here may no longer be heard but the room is full of rich and varied memories.

What an exquisite gift this building was for the staff and pupils of St Louis High School! Its role still includes prayer and music but it now incorporates all sorts of events around drama, art, meetings and classroom activity. This imaginative use of a very beautiful and sacred space is a powerful reminder of the origins and purpose of the St Louis system of education and its values, particularly in the field of music and the arts.

Detail, fleur de lis, left sanctuary.
Photo by Vincent Kennedy.

The St Louis High School staff, May 1976. Sister Kathleen O'Sullivan, principal, is centre-front, with Peggy Uí Chúilleabháin on left and Vincent Kennedy on right.

Fiana Griffin

'LA CRÈME DE LA CRÈME'

*Fiana Griffin remembers the unique combination of Peaches and cream,
and then the radical 1960s.*

The people who gave the character to the area in which St Louis was founded in 1913 were wealthy, Protestant and Unionist. Seeking a better life away from the disease-laden airs of the city on the other side of the Grand Canal, they established the independent township of Rathmines in 1847, incorporating Rathgar, Ranelagh and Milltown by the 1860s. The area was so well developed by 1860 that, as well as Rathmines Church, a second Catholic church on Rathgar Road was required to minister to the needs of the numerous Catholic servants. From the late 19th century, households of the emerging Catholic middle class also began to establish themselves there, their numbers increasing after the Irish Free State was founded in 1922, although Rathmines elected a Unionist candidate to the Dáil as late as 1929, the last constituency to do so.

In the 1950s, when I was born, quite a number of Protestants still lived quietly in the area, although in decreasing numbers. Our Presbyterian neighbours worked in Cadbury's, had a bountiful cherry tree and regaled us with the produce of both, with reserved smiles. The Catholic Church and the risen Irish people had taken the country back to make it (to quote Éamon de Valera) 'the spiritual reservoir of Europe' and the hub of a Catholic empire that would outshine that of our erstwhile rulers.

Understandably, Catholics aspired to the refinement and gentility that had once been the preserve of Protestants. At St Louis, we were constantly exhorted to be a credit to family and school by ladylike comportment. Every Tuesday we gathered in the hall for lectures on life from Sr Mary Frances Teresa (aka 'Peach', a nod to Père of St Mary's College, Rathmines). Most of her pearls of wisdom have rolled away from me but not the detailed instructions on how to allow courteous young men to remove our hats, coats and gloves from us in fine restaurants, presumably the prelude to a diamond ring as long as we kept our legs together and uncrossed. What we might do other than marry was rarely hinted at; the world of work or achievement post Leaving Certificate did not appear to be high on the agenda. We were privileged young ladies whose parents were paying for our education. In one of her most unforgettable lines, she declared that we were *'la crème de la crème'*. To be fair, she also introduced us to the old adage, 'Aim for the stars, and you might land on the roof,' although I can't remember whether the context was marriage, our relationship with Jesus or something more worldly.

The winds of change began to rock Irish society in the 1960s, but the year of the big wind in education in general, and in St Louis, Rathmines, in particular, was 1967. This was when Donogh O'Malley largely dismantled educational privilege by bringing in the free education scheme for secondary schools and

two vibrant young women doing their Higher Diplomas came to teach us fifth years. Lovely, glamorous Miss Brídín Gilroy, who could occasionally be seen on RTÉ, taught Spanish through her passion for the literature and culture of Spain. As soon as we had acquired a smattering of the language, she guided us almost blindfold through the labyrinth of Lorca's *The House of Bernarda Alba* with the constant exhortation to 'guess' when we were stymied. Occasionally, she turned up guitar in hand and had us singing popular songs. I doubt if any of her former pupils have forgotten 'Clavelitos'.

Intellectual, literary and occasionally out-rageous, Miss Ita Daly was ostensibly employed to teach us English for the Leaving Certificate but in practice she offered us the key to self-discovery as she invited us to explore the uncharted territory of our minds. She made a promise, which she kept, to spend as much time as possible on classroom discussions, her favoured method – and ours – of approaching this journey.

Those hours spent sweltering in Andalucia or engaged in urgent debate helped us to mix the cream into the milk while we aimed for the stars. I think most of us managed to land on the roof.

Pádraigín Clancy

Ó RÁTH MAOINIS GO hINIS MÓR ÁRAINN

Pádraigín Clancy attributes some of her confidence and communication skills to her education in St Louis High School.

Last year I was invited to speak at the Eucharistic Congress in Dublin on 'Wisdom and Prayer from the Gaelic Tradition'. There were three hundred people in front of me. As I looked out with a small degree of trepidation, a smiling, kindly-faced, middle-aged woman came up and spoke to me; 'I don't know will you remember me,' she said. 'I am Sr Josephine.'

Sr Josephine? I thought. Not the Sr Josephine who first taught me when I was four years of age in St Louis? A woman I had not seen since and whose kindness I clearly remembered. The years fell away. Thug an tSiúr Seosaimhín misneach dom agus mé i mo leanbh óg agus ar an ócáid speisialta sin chuir sí ríméad ar mo chroí arís agus leagadh beannacht ar mo chuid oibre. Ba bhua mór é. That was the gift of the St Louis education for me – it essentially inspired confidence rather than fear.

My entire primary and secondary education from the age of four to seventeen was with the Sisters of St Louis, so whoever I am they have been central in my formation. Thaitin liom go mór bheith ag freastal ar Ardscoil San Lughaidh. Ní hé sin le rá go raibh mo cheann ins na leabhair i gcónaí ach go raibh an-saol agam ag rith gan fhuacht gan fhaitíos timpeall na scoile in éineacht le mo chara dhíl, Anne-Marie Ahern. B'fhéidir de bharr an traidisiúin reiligiúnaigh sa scoil bhí meas mór ag na scoláirí agus na múinteoirí ar a chéile agus b'iontach an rud dúinn é. Leagadh béim ní hamháin ar an scolaíocht ach fresin ar fhorbairt iomlán an duine. Is cuimhin liom go maith i mo chéad bhliain san ardscoil, ár bpríomhoide, an tSiúr Caitlín Ní Shúilleabháin, ag cur ina luí orainn cé chomh tábhachtach agus a bhí sé sult a bhaint as an saol ar scoil.

The Louis education equipped me for life in many ways. The fact that the school was (and is) non-fee-paying engendered respect for people from all walks of life. One shared one's desk with the deprived and the privileged and quickly learnt that goodness and brilliance emerge from every quarter. It was a life lesson.

The emphasis on good communication skills through foreign language teaching, interschool debating and drama was central. Nach áthasach a bhíonn na turasóirí as an nGearmáin agus as an bhFrainc anseo ag Dún Aonghasa in Árainn nuair a chloiseann siad mo chúpla focal sa Ghearmáinis agus sa bhFraincis. Agus nach bródúil a bheadh Bean Uí Chúilleabháin agus an tSiúr Áine dá gcloisfidís iad ag moladh mo chanúint bhreá álainn sa dhá theanga!

Bhí an-ghrá agam i gcónaí don stair. Fuaireas ón gcliabhán é ar ucht mo mháthar agus ó mo mhuintir ar fad. Cuireadh leis go mór be bharr an phaisin a bhí ag ár múinteoir staraí den scoth, Eibhlín Breathnach.

Is beag an smaoineamh a bhí agam nuair a bhí mé ag plé le tionscnamh faoi shaol na mainistreach in Éirinn fadó (ábhar a bhí an-ghar do chroí Eibhlin) go mbeinn ag staidéar an ábhair chéanna san ollscoil na blianta ina dhiaidh. Tá cuid mhór de mo shaol caite agam anois ag tabhairt léachtanna, cainteanna agus cúrsaí spioradálta faoi thraidisiún na nGael, ní hamháin in Éirinn ach chomh fada ó bhaile le Meirceá agus an Astráil.

Speaking of travel. Paris will always hold a special place in my heart since I first enjoyed a marvellous week there under the guidance of the aforesaid dynamic Ms Breathnach and the ever-aesthetic Mrs Marcus. How we took the city's monuments, galleries, river and cafés by storm, dressed to 'the height of fashion' in our cowboy boots and protruding lacy undergarments.

Ach ní raibh mé ar muin na muice ar scoil gach lá! Sa rang matamaitice caitheadh isteach i measc na 'lame ducks' mé in ionad na 'flying swans'. Fresin, nuair a d'oscail mé mo bhéal le háit a fháil sa chór cáiliúil sin, Cantairí Óga Átha Cliath, dúradh liom é a dhúnadh ar an dtort le 'next please'. But all was not lost: some years later I learnt how to 'mouth' with great exactitude and good humour in Mrs Maguire's class choir. I have since learnt how to play the tin whistle and concertina.

If I wished for anything in my years in St Louis, it was for more sport. I was a good runner so I do envy the girls today the sporting options available to them, with Gaelic football and hockey having been introduced. Perhaps too, in retrospect, a little more practicality might have been no harm. While I loved Mr Kennedy's science class and recall the mystery of photosynthesis, sometimes I do wish I had had the option of taking domestic science and simply learn how to make a dress or bake a cake!

Ach ar deireadh thiar thall nuair a smaoiním siar ar mo chuid laethanta scoile agus mé ag plé le cúram an tí, tagann focail an amhráin a mhúin an tSiúr Helen Power dúinn i rang na Gaeilge aníos ó mo chroí: 'Ó labhair an teanga Gaeilge liom…' Nó focail an amhráin a chanamar le chéile sa thionól gach maidin – cloisim mé féin á gcanadh: 'Now thank we all our God with hearts and hands and voices// who wondrous things has done, in whom this world rejoices…'

Comhghairdeachas d'Ardscoil San Lughaidh ar chomóradh céad bliain. Go n-éirí go geal libh amach anseo. Guím rath Dé ar bhur gcuid oibre agus ar dheis Dé go raibh siad siúd atá imithe romhainn ar shlí na fírinne.

*Lauren McMahon as Fantine
in the 2013 production of* Les Misérables.

Brídín Gilroy

SNAPSHOTS OF THE ARTS IN ST LOUIS

Brídín Gilroy gives a taste of the music, drama and visual arts that have had pride of place in St Louis High School.

In my long experience of St Louis High School, both as pupil in the 1950s and teacher from the 1970s to the 1990s, the arts have always fitted seamlessly into the school year – choirs, orchestra, school musicals, drama and, supported by the formal curriculum, literature and the visual arts.

A production of *The Student Prince*, staged in 1954 by the senior school (as the high shool was then called) remains an early, magical memory from my years as a pupil of the junior school, then located in Numbers 7 and 8 Grosvenor Road. We were brought, along with the rest of the school (senior and junior), to see the dress rehearsal in the new concert hall, then known as Assumpta Hall. In those pre-internet, pre-

television years, I was totally enchanted by the glamour of the occasion: the music, the performances of Mary Cahill as the prince and Lolita Bracken – for several years the shining star of musical productions in the school – in the role of Kathie, the barmaid with whom the prince has fallen in love.

I went on to sing the Hallelujah Chorus many times with Our Lady's Choral Society in its annual performance of *Messiah* but nothing matched the challenge of learning that wonderful chorus and the thrill of performing it for the first time with the school choir under the baton of the redoubtable Sr Clothilde, choirmistress *extraordinaire* in St Louis throughout the 1940s and 1950s. Decades later, in

2006, this achievement was surpassed by a performance, to great acclaim, of *The Messiah* (school's version) in full, by the choirs of St Louis Rathmines and St Louis Carrickmacross. The performance, which was conducted by Sr Pauline Johnson, was held in the Church of the Three Patrons, Rathgar.

The school orchestra has always been an important part of the St Louis musical scene. In my schooldays, it was conducted by Sr Fulgentia (later Sr Mary Finan) and was an after-school activity for those playing or learning to play musical instruments. Although I never progressed beyond the back row of the second fiddles, lost in admiration for leader Ursula Hough, playing with such panache up front, this was my introduction to the orchestral repertoire. To this day, whenever I hear Mozart's *Eine Kleine Nachtmusik* or the ballet music from Schubert's *Rosamunde* overture, I find myself humming the line of the second fiddles!

The arts continued to flourish, with exciting additional activities, through the last decades of the 20th century, by which time I had returned to the school as a teacher. Iris Maguire brought choral singing to a new level of excellence through the 1970s and St Louis won awards including the Fallon Cup for plainchant and the Turner Huggard Cup for three-part choirs. Mrs Maguire instituted a school choral festival,

a competition that took place annually at the Halloween mid-term break. The final was judged by external adjudicators – professional musicians, among them Brian Ó Dubhghaill, sadly recently deceased, former music inspector and director of the Cantairí Óga Átha Cliath. This choir, which originated in St Louis Primary School, performed and competed for more than fifty years with outstanding success at concerts and choral festivals, nationally and internationally, and many of its members continued to sing with the Cantairí Óga throughout their years in St Louis High School. Mrs Maguire's choirs and choral festival produced such influential practitioners and teachers of music as Gráinne Gormley, conductor of the famous choir of Clarendon Street Church, Anne Leahy, organist and lecturer in music at DIT until her untimely death, and Andreja Malir, harpist with the RTÉ Symphony Orchestra. Meanwhile, numerous primary teachers pass their gift of music on to new generations.

With a list of productions too numerous to mention, the school musical has been the showcase for so much talent down the years that I can pick, as from a lucky bag, only one musical from the past and applaud the centenary production of *Les Misérables*. Out of the bag, from the 1980s, comes *The King and I*. How well I remember Mary Purcell as a delightful Anna and, in the role of Tuptim,

Above: Cosette (Hazel Nolan) and Marius (Matthew Ambrose) visit Valjean (Roy Grimson) after their wedding.

Below: 'Master of the House' chorus with Fionntán Larney and Michaela Roche as Monsieur et Madame Thénardier.

the king's slave, Siobhán McCarthy, who went on to star in *Mama Mia, Evita* and other hit musicals and plays in the West End. *The King and I* was one of many memorable musicals produced by Máire Cranny, with musical direction by Iris Maguire.

In October of the centenary year of 2013, St Louis High School staged *Les Misérables,* in collaboration with the students of St Mary's College, Rathmines. A challenging work to perform by any standards, this spectacular production by Bernard Lynch with musical direction by Ray Ryan will long be remembered as a highlight of the year's celebrations.

The drama festival, for which I had responsibility, filled the gap in the years when there was no musical and was very popular throughout the 1980s. Each year group produced short plays or scenes from a full-length play that were staged over three nights, excitement building up to the announcement of prizewinners by the adjudicator – for many years Jimmy McClatchie – on the last night. The festival was a major exercise in collaboration, achieved with the generous support of members of staff, parents and past pupils, many of whom produced plays, as did distinguished visiting producers, while Dympna Cullen and Caroline Gaynor of the art department played an indispensable role in overseeing the creation of sets.

In 1988, with the support and encouragement of the then principal, Sr Eithne Woulfe, the drama festival was succeeded by an arts week, inspired by a visit I made to Clifden (County Galway) Arts Week. Now a national arts festival, it had its origins in Clifden Community School where its founder, Brendan Flynn, was a teacher. For its fortunate students, the school continues to be a primary focus of the festival. Over the years, the St Louis version of Clifden has hosted 'all kinds of everything' (and everybody) from the world of the arts – poets, novelists, artists in stained glass, rock bands, dance companies, theatre companies, classical music recitals and the ever-popular fashion show! Spearheaded by Dympna Cullen and Caroline Gaynor, the fashion show gave full rein to the creativity of the students, who were presented with the task of creating outfits using recycled materials, often producing some quite sensational results.

Since her arrival in the school in 1993 the dynamic Clíona McDonough has introduced significant innovations in music education, as well as continuing established traditions such as the school musical and the now three-day arts festival. The choral exchange with Hunterhouse College, Belfast, which she established in 2000, fosters cross-border understanding between young people, as they experience the joy and excitement of joint performances. The annual spring concert provides opportunities for first years to perform a full cantata and for instrumental players to display their talents. Music performance is an integral part of all major school events and was at the core of the centenary celebrations of 2013-14.

2013 was the year of other Rathmines centenaries and St Louis High School entered the domain of national centenaries with its participation in the creation of the wonderful *1913 Lockout Tapestry,* involving artists Cathy Henderson, Robert Ballagh and a variety of community groups. Twenty students represented St Louis High School, joining students from Larkin Community College and Mater Dei Primary School, Basin Lane, in creating the final panel of the tapestry, described by Cathy Henderson as her favourite, featuring the torch of hope carried into the future. Congratulations to those students on a unique achievement, to Caroline Gaynor of the art department in St Louis and to Angela Keane, who liaised with the schools on behalf of the tapestry project.

The nurturing of creativity through education in the arts has always been a basic tenet of the St Louis philosophy of education and has laid the foundation for a lifetime of practice, or simply pure enjoyment of the arts for generations of girls who passed through St Louis High School over the past century. We express our gratitude to successive generations of the Sisters of St Louis for facilitating these life-enhancing educational opportunities.

Peggy Bean Uí Chúilleabháin

AN tSIÚR CAITLÍN NÍ SHÚILLEABHÁIN

Cuimhníonn Peggy Bean Uí Chúilleabháin ar phríomhoide ceannróideach (1970-76) a dhein mórán chun an ardscoil a chur chun cinn ins na seachtóidí.

Rugadh an tSiúr Caitlín i dTamhnach an tSalainn (Mountcharles) – sráidbhaile beag i dTír Chonaill – sa bhliain 1920. Cé gur thaisteal sí i bhfad óna háit dúchais i rith a saoil, ní dhearna sí dearmad riamh ar an mbaile agus d'fhill sí ar a contae dúchais go minic ar cuairt chuig gaolta nó ar laethanta saoire cois farraige. Ba gheal léi i gcónaí an fharraige!

Ceapadh an tSiúr Caitlín mar phríomhoide in Ardscoil San Lughaidh Ráth Maonais sa bhliain 1970. Ón gcéad lá, thug sí faoin a post le fonn agus díograis! Ba dhúshlán mór é, ag an am, ach cinnte bhí na buanna riachtanacha aici. Bean fíor-chumasach, dícheallach, bháúil agus ghealgháireach ab ea í.

Thuig an tSiúr Caitlín gurb é muintir na scoile – daltaí, múinteoirí, tuismitheoirí, foireann riaracháin, na hoibrithe tacaíochta go léir – an gné is tábhachtaí a bhaineann le scoil. Chuir sí aithne ar gach duine gan mhoill. Chuir sí timpeallacht ar fáil a chabhraigh le fás agus forbairt dearfach.

Thosaigh sí ag pleanáil todhchaí iontach don scoil. B'í a chuir tús le na cainteanna leis an Roinn Oideachais chun foirgneamh nua-aimseartha a thógáil – foirgneamh atá le feiceáil inniu. Rinne sí teagmháil le scoileanna taobh amuigh den tír agus d'eagraigh sí malartú scoile leis an bhFrainc agus an nGearmáin. Mar sin bhí an deis ag múinteoirí agus daltaí dul thar lear agus cultúr eile a bhlaiseadh agus teanga iasachta a fhoghlaim gan mórán dua. B'í a bhí i gcónaí ag féachaint chuige go raibh Ardscoil San Lughaidh chun tosaigh agus páirteach i ngach tionscnamh fiúntach nua. Le linn a réim ghlac an scoil páirt i scéim phíolótach na hidirbhliana atá fós ar fáil dos na daltaí inniu – bliain scoile bhreise a roghnaíonn formhór na ndaltaí, bliain saor ó scrúdaithe agus ó chúinsí an churaclaim.

Cé a dhéanfadh dearmad ar na tionóil aeracha a stiúraigh sí gach uile mhaidin sa halla? Bhíodh ceol agus craic ar siúl chomh maith le paidreacha agus fógraí an lae! (Nach mise a bhíodh neirbhíseach aon uair nach mbíodh sí in ann a bheith i láthair agus mise mar leas-phríomhoide ag iarraidh a háit a ghlacadh.) Sa tslí sin thosaigh na daltaí an lá scoile go fonnmhar! Thosaigh sí an córas tí (house system) le múinteoirí mar mháistreás tí agus mar mháistreás ranga i bhfeighil gach bliainghrúpa. De bharr an chórais seo mhothaigh na daltaí níos sona sa scoil. Bhí go leor deiseanna difriúla ar fáil dos na daltaí páirt a ghlacadh i gceoldrámaí, drámaí, cór agus réimse mór imeachtaí spóirt.

Go luath bhí seomra foirne fairsing againn, cruinnithe míosúla agus deis againn cúrsaí scoile a phlé. Ba mhinic a thug an tSiúr Caitlín cuireadh dúinn bualadh isteach léi ina hoifig, chun cúrsaí pearsanta a phlé. D'fhéach sí chuige léachtanna suimiúla a chur ar fáil

agus múinteoirí a ligeadh amach ar chúrsaí oideachasúla – imeachtaí le leas na múinteoirí agus na scoile.

Ní dhearna sí faillí ar ról tábhachtach na dtuismitheoirí i saol na scoile. Bhunaigh sí coiste na dtuistí chun deis a thabhairt dóibh a bheith gníomhach agus páirteach i saol na scoile. Uair sa bhliain bhíodh cruinniú ag na tuismitheoirí le múinteoirí a bpáistí chun cúrsaí scoile a phlé agus ó am go ham bhíodh oíche siamsaíochta againn go léir sa halla.

D'éirigh leis an tSiúr Caitlín go leor spriocanna eile a bhaint amach le linn a tréimhse in oifig. Mar shampla bunaíodh coiste na ndaltaí, a thug deis dóibh a gcuid tuairimí a chur in iúl agus fíorpháirt a ghlacadh i riaradh na scoile. Osclaíodh oifig sa scoil le rúnaí lánaimseartha agus duine i mbun cúrsaí airgid – beirt a bhí fíorthábhachtach i saol na scoile.

Samhradh na bliana 1976 d'fhág an tSiúr Caitlín slán le hArdscoil San Lughaidh agus sna blianta ina dhiaidh sin, chaith sí tréimhsí i Sasana agus i Meiriceá ag staidéar agus ag obair mar chomhairleoir agus stiúrthóir cúrsaí spioradálta. Bhain sí taitneamh agus sásamh as an tréimhse seo ina saol.

D'fhill an tSiúr Caitlín ar Bhaile Átha Cliath agus níor chuir sé iontas dá laghad ar aon duine gur lean sí ar aghaidh ag obair. Seoladh a leabhar *Light Out of Darkness* in 1993. Bhí suim aici i gcónaí in Ardscoil San Lughaidh agus ba mhinic a thug sí cuairt orainn sa seomra foirne, chun caint agus comhrá a dhéanamh. Fuair sí bás ar an 25ú Iúil 2007.

Go ndéana Dia trócaire ar a hanam. Duine ar leith ab ea an tSiúr Caitlín – i dtús áite bean rialta, duine diaganta, scoláire, múinteoir spreagúil, comhairleoir báúil, ceannródaí éifeachtach a chuaigh go mór i gcion ar dhaoine, idir óg agus aosta. Nach raibh an t-ádh dearg orainne go raibh sí linn mar phríomhoide ins na blianta sin?

Buskers, left to right: Mary Elliott (violin), Barbara McHugh (flauto busho), Cecily O'Flynn (stringed racquet), Ann O'Sullivan (cello). Conductor: Helen O'Meehan. All Leaving Certificate class, May 1963.

Máire Cosgrove

BIG SCHOOL

Bhí imní orm an chéad lá
Ach ba eachtra duitse é.
Chloígh mé leat!
Níos déanaí, nuair a chaill mé
Eochair mo thaisceadáin
D'iarr mé ort teacht liom
Don gceann bliana
Chun an bhreiseochair a fháil.

Cúpla bliain ina dhiaidh
Bhí córas eile i bhfeidhm,
A glas féin ag gach dalta.
Nuair a cailleadh d'eochairse
Bhí sé go nádúrtha dul le chéile
Freddie a lorg
Go ngearrfadh sé lúb an ghlais.

Thángamar air taobh leis an halla,
Ag an doras caol san
Nach n-osclaítear ach go hannamh,
Ina sheasamh go ciúin, ciúin
Ag breathnú amach.
D'fhéachamar thar a ghualainn.

Bhí sionnach óg ag stánadh ar ais air.
Dhá shúil órga bhuí
Faoi scáth na sceithe.

Nóiméad fada,
Ceathrar mar dhealbha,
Ansin d'iompaigh sé agus d'imigh.

Tá Freddie ar shlí na fírinne anois
Agus, an tseachtain seo chugainn,
Rachaidh ár mbeirt iníon
Isteach sa chéad bhliain
Agus iad araon ag súil leis.

Tá gach rud réidh do mo Bhríd, measaim,
Sliabh beag d'éadaí agus leabhair,
Mála scoile agus gach a théann ann,
Agus glas breá loinnreach práis
Chun súil a choimeád ar a taisceadán,
Súil órga bhuí.

Jessica Traynor

TREASURE

When I was very young I realised
that grown-ups hide their treasure
and so I'd search the corners
of our overgrown garden,
pick through brambles in the back lane,
push fingers into crannies in the granite
    walls.

Things I found but have since lost:
a rusted lump of cast-iron wreathed in
    flowers,
a glass bottle-stopper worn smooth
as if by water. A robin's nest, abandoned,
a knot-hole groove in the bannister
the perfect fit for my thumb.

Somewhere, there is a map
to the place these things are hidden.
It may be buried in this flower bed
among a thousand smashed tea-cups
or folded in this book like a bus ticket
that, when falling, whispers keep looking.

2013

Yvonne Jerrold

IMAGES

It begins with images,
with shadows that I cannot see,
drifting at the edges of my mind,
until I turn to face them,
and they flee;

images so swift
that vanish in a blink
of fleeting light I cannot catch…

But images of what? I cannot tell;
of everything I do not know,
everything I cannot think
and nothing to be done;

of someone curled up on the ground,
trying not to make a sound;

of hands and arms and locks and walls
and footsteps padding back and forth;

of faces pressed against the door
and someone madder locked inside,

and hearing voices…

1998

Nessa O'Mahony

POLISH

The first break;
a morning's weight
of geometry,
chalk lacing air.
A door knock,
an imperceptible nod
and we're off,
a work party of four,
wine sleeves rolled up.
The concert hall waits,
half-lit through side windows,
notes of past performances
ringing in our ears.
We know the score,
prepare our instruments:
yellow duster cloths
walked back and forth,
stage to door,
across the beeswax
till the timber glistens
our reflections back at us.

No spit, but we are artists
of the polish,
practising the perfect
that will last us
all our lives.

Autumn 1977

Una Mangan and her sister Claire.

Ita Daly

'I WAS HAPPY THERE'

Ita Daly talks to Una Mangan, who came to St Louis High School in 1931
from the 'distant environs' of Bloomfield Avenue, and hated leaving it.

Una Mangan, who started secondary school in 1931, is among the most senior of the St Louis High School past pupils. When I phoned her she told me that she was happy to talk about her memories of her schooldays and I am now sitting in her garden in the summer sun. I notice how elegant she is and how gracefully I am being received.

I am impressed by her recall but it is a phrase that she uses and repeats that catches my attention.

'I was happy there,' she says.

When she started in the high school there were seven girls in her class. She wasn't a local girl but came from the distant environs of Bloomfield Avenue.

'But I had cousins living on Rathgar Road who had gone to the high school so I went too.'

'Do you remember any of your teachers?'

'There was Miss Hayes. And Miss Stuart taught us maths. And, of course, Sr Clothilde for music. Music was very important in the school.'

Una played the cello in the orchestra and her sister, Claire, who later became a St Louis Sister, played the violin.

For the Eucharistic Congress in 1932 she was part of a special schools' choir.

'Music was always important. We'd be taken out of class to practise for the musicals. Sr Denise started me on the cello and in 1937 the orchestra was runner-up in the Father Matthew

Feis. Claire and I entered the feis too, singing duets.' Sport was important also, with both camogie and hockey being played.

Una remembers the 'new' school being built [1950]. 'Our classrooms were in Sacred Heart [8 Grosvenor Road] and I used to have the job of locking up – it was a big responsibility.'

And it was during her day that the uniform changed from navy to wine and the school became all-Irish. She studied Irish, English, Maths, History and Geography for her Leaving Certificate.

'There was no exam centre in the school; we had to go down to St Mary's. There was a centre in the library also, as far as I remember.'

She hated leaving school. 'I cried when I had to leave – lots of us did. The nuns were so easy to talk to and get along with. Nobody was afraid of them.'

When she smiles I can see her retreating back into those years.

'At lunchtime we'd go down to Rathmines to get something to eat. I played tennis...I was happy there.'

'And what did you do when you left?'

She smiles again. 'I managed to stay on for another year. At the top of Sacred Heart there were commercial classes and I did a secretarial course there. I think the reason I did it was so that I could stay in St Louis for an extra year.'

Una Mangan today, still a St Louis girl.

Ann-Marie Madigan.

Ann-Marie Madigan

PORTRAIT
OF A SCIENTIST

*Ann-Marie Madigan is a past pupil who literally reaches for the stars
in her research, having taken in India, Southeast Asia,
Central America and California along the way.*

I am a NASA Einstein Fellow in the theoretical astrophysics department of the University of California, Berkeley.

I discovered my love of maths and physics in the classrooms of St Louis, becoming particularly interested in mechanics and the orbits of planets around stars. I was also an active member of the athletics club, portfolio class and the Cantairí Óga Átha Cliath.

I did my Leaving Certificate in 2000 and moved to Galway, where I spent four years studying physics and astronomy in NUIG and had exceptional fun. In term time I kept busy studying and going out with friends and picking up new activities such as karate and yoga. In my free time I developed a love of travelling, back-packing through Southeast Asia and central America.

I graduated in 2004 and at that point I took a year's break from study to travel to India, where I worked as a teacher for a Tibetan charity and nurtured my love of yoga and delicious food. I beat typhoid and narrowly avoided the tsunami that hit the Indian coastline, to come back to Ireland in 2005.

I then moved to the Netherlands to do a two-year research Masters in Astronomy in Leiden University. In Leiden I joined the theoretical astrophysics group, working with two supervisors on the dynamics of stars near supermassive black holes. I completed my masters in 2007 and the Netherlands Organisation for Scientific Research gave me a fellowship to continue my work. I was awarded a PhD in Astronomy in 2012 for my research on stellar dynamics and subsequently received an Einstein post-doctoral fellowship with NASA.

Currently I am a member of the theoretical astrophysics department in the University of California, Berkeley, researching how stars move and interact with one another near supermassive black holes. These stars can form in disks around the black holes, like planets form in disks around stars. If they get too close to the black holes, they can be ripped apart or even swallowed whole. I have published papers on the theoretical mechanisms by which this happens and I collaborate in research with observers of the centre of our galaxy where there lies a supermassive black hole with a mass of four million suns.

I live just outside San Francisco but love coming back home to Dublin as often as I can.

Cuisle 'pelican' window by David Willis.

Jewellery by Sadhbh McCormack.

Sadhbh McCormack

I ALWAYS WANTED TO BE AN ARTIST

Sadhbh McCormack followed in her mother's artistic footsteps by becoming a jewellery designer but like her father chose to work in the commercial world.

My parents gave me the choice of where I wanted to go to secondary school. I chose St Louis because there was nobody else I knew going there. I didn't want to follow the crowd. I was seduced by the thought of starting a new life and growing up on my own. Somehow, at the age of twelve, I knew that St Louis was the school that would allow me to become the independent, free-spirited, strong individual I wanted to grow into.

The diversity of the students in the school attracted me also. Girls from totally different backgrounds, cultures, upbringing and values were all brought together in an accepting and open way. We respected one another from the start and we learned to get along and eventually love and enjoy the differences that set us apart. I believe it was this respect and this acceptance of difference that allowed each of us girls to be ourselves and to become what we wanted to be as individuals.

During my Leaving Certificate year I was torn between business and art for my college education. My father is a businessman and my mother, Jane Proctor, is a successful artist. I knew my heart was made for art and design but a huge part of me liked the idea of a good life, making money in the business world and being a savvy career woman. I chose art, much to the secret delight of both my parents, as they believed I should pursue my talent.

My mother, Jane, continues to draw and paint in her studio in Rathmines. She also teaches – in fact she taught art in St Louis for a couple of years at one time and as a result has always been an admirer of the school. She exhibits her work both in Ireland and internationally and designed and made a book illustrating the poems of Seamus Heaney that is in the National Library in Dublin. Her work is also part of many permanent collections, including that of Boston College. She has always been passionate about art and her whole life has been involved in making it and teaching it.

I spent four years studying in the National College of Art and Design. I grew into a strong young woman with a vision of how I wanted my life to be. I wanted to go to the Royal College of Art in London the moment I heard about it. I knew I would do this eventually but there were times when I thought it would never happen. I found my twenties a challenging time. In a way I was more confident at school. College throws a lot of confusion your way. There is a lot of pressure to succeed, to achieve, to perform and to follow conventions at the same time.

I loved making and I have always had a passion for jewellery so I chose to study silver-smithing and jewellery in NCAD. Sometimes I think I might have preferred graphics or textiles but I continued with my craft and graduated with first class honours.

After graduating I quickly got a position in Appleby's jewellery in Dublin city. I progressed to the workshop after a few months and delighted in learning from the seven master craftsmen there.

After a while Dublin began to close in on me. The time came for me to leave and spread my wings in a new city. I chose London and within four days of making the decision I left my job, packed a suitcase for the summer and made my way to east London where my two friends, Adam and Mark, were living. The three of us shared their dingy two-bedroom apartment for a few months until we found a place for the three of us to live. This was the beginning of my London adventure and when I look back on all the people, parties, dinners, weekends, money stresses and awful jobs, it feels like a lifetime ago.

I soon realised that looking for work in design was difficult and competitive. I applied to do a masters in the Royal College of Art and was accepted. I had to make this happen financially so I worked as a cocktail waitress in Covent Garden for a year. I earned stupendous cash as head cocktail waitress and managed to keep this job through my two years at college. It was an intense time. I became obsessed with design, designers and everything within the innovation bubble. I graduated, exhausted, burnt out and in need of something less consuming.

Right: Jewellery by
Sadhbh McCormack.

Below: Painting by
Jane Proctor.

I left the college with the knowledge that I wanted to pursue my career in the industry/ commercial side of jewellery. Maybe my dream of combining business with art was actually beginning to come true.

Immediately I got a job working as the creative assistant at Annoushka in Chelsea. Annoushka is a high-profile brand, creating unique jewellery that is exclusive and exquisite and also worn for everyday casual glamour. I enjoy the fancy parties I attend through work; I often find myself at gorgeous west London boutiques for drinks receptions. But it is east London that really holds my heart. I live in Hackney with great friends and feel totally at home there. I adore the area, the feeling, the food, markets, bars, outdoor lidos, galleries, boutiques, events, parties and the fact that all my best friends are around me, including my sister, Anna. East London is where I feel most calm, easy, inspired and happy.

I believe it is important to spread your wings, leave home early and live in an international city. Everyone should travel and experience the world, meet people from different places and different cultures and develop their own views and opinions. I believe this enriches life, adding value, respect, knowledge and power. Leaving home is a hard option, yet very fulfilling.

My mom always had an abstract way of looking at things. I suppose I have inherited this from her. St Louis not only allowed abstract ways of thinking but encouraged and supported them.

I do miss living near my family; it is hard to be apart from family goings-on. Having my sister in London makes the world of difference. I am a home bird at heart and I can miss my mom and dad a lot. I have a very close relationship with my mom and I hope that in the future I won't be apart from her so much. Having been inspired by her all my life, I can see that I am the person I am today because of how she nurtured me and taught me to be strong. Confidence without arrogance was what she tried to instil in both her girls and I greatly respect her for the way she has influenced my take on the world.

I am in London to achieve something. I am not sure I will know when I have achieved it but I am going to see my vision through. I still have my dreams and an idea of what I want to get out of life in a few years. I am working hard, I am enjoying myself and I'm thinking maybe Paris next.

Sadhbh is now a designer for Solange Azagury Partridge.

Sadhbh McCormack (left) and Jane Proctor.

Photo by Dominick Walsh, courtesy of Anne Enright.

Anne Enright

HAVING A LAUGH

Among many other things, novelist Anne Enright learned in school that 'beauty is all at the edges', that no two St Louis Sisters were the same and to 'get on with it'.

The sight and sound of a choir of girls still makes the tears hop out of my eyes: that mixture of harmony and difference, each girl working her look as best she can with jewellery or attitude, a hairband or earrings, an expression on her face that says, 'This is me, OK?' What makes me so sentimental? Growth and control. It is the feeling of girls becoming individuals and remaining a force, both at the same time.

This I realised at a concert, shortly before I sent my own daughter to a single-sex school. How could I do this to her? a former Louis girl asked me. 'She'll fall in love with the first man she meets.' And it is true that I fell in love very soon after I left school: these are powerful years. I don't know why I wanted to see my daughter singing alto, in her turn, or wearing a uniform,

or seeing boys as a separate species for a while. I suppose I wanted her to experience that same mix of sweetness and power the choir brought back to me. I wanted to give her space.

These days, space is harder to find. There is Facebook and ask.fm, screen grabs and selfies, there is waggling your ass and much war paint and goddamn Hollister. It might always have been like this, in some essential way, but it is all out there now, named, shamed and shouty: it's all a bit bare. My daughter's memories of school are codified as soon as they happen. Sometimes the photo of the good time is more important than the good time. When I think of my years in St Louis there is, perhaps by contrast, a vague, interior feel to it all.

Brass stair rails, the speckled green and yellow

of terrazzo floors and steps: I remember the particular blue of the crest in the main hall – something to look at during assembly. School is a great place for distraction. Every morning I walked over and between the roots of a huge magnolia tree that spread through the yard and when sixth year came I was able to look out over the top of it, in flower. I loved this tree although I did not call it 'love' at the time and I loved the corridor of glass down to the scented chapel. If distraction teaches us anything, it is that beauty is all at the edges.

Or am I too nostalgic? The smell of furniture polish is what I remember, although the truth of school buildings is that they smell used; sandwiches, leaky bottles of milk, apple cores. I remember a faint pong of gas as you passed the science lab, a bit of damp in there maybe, a basement mix of sweet and sour, but it is not wet gabardine I recall so much as the smell, under the iron, of the cotton polyester blouses we wore and the bubbles that never came out of the reinforced collar. I remember inhaling new books, putting my nose right down in there along the crease and hauling it in.

The herringbone pattern I first saw on the parquet in the national school still holds a fascination, after a childhood we spent polishing it by sliding along on waxy cloths. It was by the two steps on this apparently endless corridor that Sr Madeline knelt down beside

me, a late addition in high babies. She held me by the shoulders and looked at me, then kissed me and told me I was very welcome. I was five years old. Sr Madeline had long, heavy skirts with rosary beads suspended from a wide, leather belt. A passionate, brown-eyed woman, her upper lip was dark with hair – that was another thing I noticed, when she sank down in her heavy skirts and took me in her arms, when I was five years old. My mother wore a hat for the occasion. It was 1967.

I met a very upper class English lady once with the deepest voice you could imagine and, when I told her I was educated by nuns in Ireland, she asked, in a sort of velvety growl, 'And were they terribly sadistic?'

'Well, no,' I said (though I did not like to disappoint). 'They were, you know, themselves.'

The sense I had of the Louis nuns was not one of uniformity but of difference; they were women of character and personality. Some of them were made small by the life and others were made more clear by it and they were worked according to their strengths by the management of the day. My first two teachers, Sr Scholastica and Sr Rumold, were endlessly gentle, sweet-hearted women who adored little children, perhaps because they had renounced their own maternal desires. The push of this melancholy is what I remember from the nuns who taught me in St Louis – how ambitious they were for us, now they had left ambition behind.

There were few enough nuns teaching by the time I left. In 1979 the country was just at the beginning of the great screeching we now call the Leaving Certificate. Our teachers resisted it as best they could, but we wore them down ('But Miss!! This isn't going to be any use for our Leaving Certificate!') The sixteen-year-old girls of Ireland have a lot to answer for. The fact that we had to fight to be taught to the test says everything about our teachers, who had zero interest, as far as I can recall, in turning out a bunch of lovely Irish girls. There was no fake piety in the classrooms of St Louis. (I do remember an amount of it during assemblies, but there was always the blue of the crest to distract, the sigh of the parting crowd as a girl fainted at the back.)

If anything there was a kind of impatience from the teachers that was part, I think, of the restlessness of the changing world outside. Oh, come on! (Sr Mairéad); Get on with it! (Mrs Marcus, Mrs Supple); Stop talking nonsense! (Mrs Slattery, Mr Kennedy); Grab the world by the throat; it is yours! (All of them, Betty especially). They had such belief, when you think about it. No one was telling us to get back in our box or look demure. No one ever suggested that true fulfilment lay in a nicely risen Victoria sponge.

There were so many things we did not know in 1979, like girls who had troubles at home of a kind that could not be discussed in those days, when many things were barely knowable. I sometimes feel we were the generation that lived the change that happened in Ireland over the last thirty years and that it wasn't easy, but was made possible, in a way, by the teachers of St Louis who fitted us for the future and not for the past.

And I think about Mrs Collins, in sixth class, who sent me off to cut up two circles into pie shapes and come back with a measurement for the circumference, which turned out to be $2\pi r$. Whatever way she managed it, it was as though the calculation had never been made before and it was as though I had discovered it all by myself. I can see the little pie slices stuck down on the page, in yellow and alternating pastel pink, and God almighty, who'da thunk it, all the pies making $2\pi r$. I was eleven years old and Mrs Collins was a great teacher and she made me feel, for a whole glorious afternoon, that, after this, I could do anything.

Julie-Anne Finan

TEN YEARS
SINCE ST LOUIS

A spell in Brazil led Julie Finan to discover her true vocation — food. Now a well-travelled gastronome, she is carving out a career in culinary entrepreneurship.

At several stages in the past ten years, I found myself living in different countries…Holland, Italy, Brazil and currently Spain. For me, a holiday of a couple of days was never long enough; I was only getting used to a place when it was time to pack up and go. Travel has always been on the itinerary and, more so, living in a different country, absorbing the culture and language.

After leaving St Louis, I set off for a career in the arts, studying fine art in IADT in Dún Laoghaire. But the life-drawing classes I had enjoyed so much in Ms Cullen's art room didn't compare to the hustle and bustle of the contemporary art world and after a chance encounter with a Brazilian photographer I left and became her assistant. This introduced me not only to the world of professional photography but to Brazilian culture. Being her assistant for the year paid off with a trip to Africa to shoot on safari and it was here, as a result of a serious but thankfully lucky car accident that I decided to review my life and focus in on what I really wanted to do. For me, photography entailed too much time in front of the computer, but cheffing, a job that had been in the background ever since I had a part-time job in my brother-in-law's kitchen at the age of sixteen, suddenly seemed like an interesting prospect – working with my hands with an end product that has some value. Everybody has to eat, right?

I took an intensive four-month course at Fáilte Ireland and, with my still shiny work shoes and neckerchief, went looking for work in Dublin. I passed by Yamamori with its 'chefs wanted' sign in the window and thought, why not? Seven years later, it's still a part of my life and I'm proud to work with an amazing and varied team of people. For me it has been a non-stop learning process.

During these years, I returned to study, first completing my national cookery apprenticeship in DIT and then, after a brief stint working in a traditional seaside kitchen in Brazil, I entered the third of a four-year degree in culinary entrepreneurship. It was hard returning to study after having worked for so long but at twenty-six I was ready for it and hungry to learn more about the growing culinary world. After I had completed third year, a chance email from my head chef ended up with my winning one of ten places on a five-month culinary scholarship to study Spanish gastronomy in Spain. Not only did I get to work with chefs from all over the world, I interned at a two-star Michelin restaurant, worked with the team from El Bulli and will get to dine at the number one restaurant in the world, El Cellar de Can Roca, in Girona. The course will conclude with a tapa competition where I show off what I have learned in the past few months – which I can tell you is a mountain of new information, experiences, cultures, languages and unforgettable memories.

Once back in Dublin, I will finish my course and plan to do a masters in food business and marketing. With my knowledge of Spanish and Portuguese, I look to working with Irish markets abroad. I know the Irish restaurant industry is at an exciting stage and big changes are ahead for the way the world views Irish cuisine. I want to be involved in this development. I believe our potential is enormous, what with our natural resources and a plethora of Irish culinary talent of international calibre. I look forward to the next ten years of learning, growing, developing future prospects – and, of course, travelling and eating my way around the world.

Iseult Deane

WALKING THROUGH SCHOOL, 2013

The everyday becomes history in Iseult Deane's reflection.

I like walking through school when everyone else is in class. I like seeing it when everyone's busy, when it's all properly happening, instead of just between classes, as your perspective on things is different when you're behind a group of second years who've all simultaneously dropped their pencil cases on the stairs.

I like walking down the first-year corridor, away from debating practice in the library and the thrum of all the computers in both computer rooms working at once on German and puzzles and history project research. I smell baking from the home economics rooms as soon as I turn the corner into the next corridor and see a third year run up from the art rooms to dry part of her T-shirt print under the hand dryers.

I walk down past the staffroom, past choir practice in the hall and transition years doing some kind of project work in the canteen. I gather that poster-making is involved, as one of them runs past me looking frustrated, carrying a pair of scissors and three markers missing lids, with glitter glue in her hair. I go through the foyer, past a basketball match in the gym and past science labs where groups of students are fidgeting with their safety glasses, visibly disappointed that nothing's supposed to explode during this class.

But my favourite part of the school is the 'old school', the three levels of classrooms built behind the hall, which have been there longer than anywhere else. It's the part with the most history, the most stories – the unexplained handprints in the paint on the staircase, the time in first year your friend said a ghost pushed her down the stairs, the rumour that the intercoms are still two-way.

This is the part of the school that makes me feel like I'm part of a story, the next chapter in a one-hundred-year-long book. It's a history: you're part of something that's still being written and you're closest to the rest of the story in the old school.

Eventually I do have to go back to class and learn about trigonometry or Shakespeare or photosynthesis. Then I'm not reading the story any longer; I'm in a class full of people writing their own Chapter 100: 'St Louis in 2013'.

Iseult Deane.

Mary Newman

2014: STILL THE 'BEAUTIFUL ENTERPRISE'

English teacher Mary Newman looks back at some of the changes
that have taken place in her twenty years on the staff of St Louis High School.

There is no environment more live and immediate than that of a school. We exist in the moment, responding to the demands of a rapidly changing society and students who are often one step ahead of us in their relationship with constantly evolving technology. At the same time, we endeavour to hold on to what's important, to be true to the vision of those who went before us and gave us a strong foundation on which to build. Having worked for twenty years as a teacher in St Louis High School, I'd like to look back on my time here and reflect on the changes that have brought us to our present incarnation – that of a vibrant, modern school, well equipped for 21st-century life – and at the same time explore whether we are still the 'high-class secondary day school' described in the original prospectus of 1913.

Sr Eithne Woulfe was principal when I came to St Louis in 1993. A Louis girl to her core, she presided over a period of unprecedented growth and development in the school. Her tenure as principal followed those of Sisters Eilís Ní Thiarnaigh and Anne Murray, who had contributed so much in terms of expanding both the physical environment and the vision of the school. Some of Sr Eithne's initiatives were quite prescient, in particular the links she fostered with the local community, St Mary's

College and Hunterhouse College in Belfast. European projects were dear to her heart and she encouraged staff members to take part in programmes that took us to Greece, Denmark, France, Luxembourg, Germany and Finland. She was outward looking and forward looking, traits that are happily embedded in the culture of our school right up to the present day. We see this in action in many ways: constant staff development and planning, participation in cutting-edge educational initiatives such as piloting the Whole School Evaluation (WSE) process and our recent membership of the network driven by the National Council for Curriculum and Assessment for reform of the Junior Cycle curriculum. Our consciousness of the world beyond our walls can be seen in the highly successful Súil Eile week, our links with St Louis in Kano, Nigeria, cross-border Horizons and the many charitable and fundraising activities that staff and students engage in every year. Sr Eithne's legacy also includes many of the staff members she appointed, a dedicated and professional group of educators who continue to guide and inform the school's vision.

In 2000 Eilís Humphreys was appointed as our first permanent lay principal. She brought with her a big national picture from her background in the transition-year support service. She encouraged staff members to take part in the TL21 programme based in NUI Maynooth, which introduced new and exciting teaching and learning methodologies to the classroom. Eilís loved to see teachers engaging in further education and embracing leadership roles. Her keen awareness of national trends and developments ensured that St Louis High School was always up to date with modern thinking and practice.

At the same time, Eilís really valued the school's Catholic ethos and traditions, an attitude that remains to this day and is evident in the thoughtful, detailed planning by our religious education department of school Masses, retreats and liturgies. In 2002, the arts centre Cuisle was opened and continues to be a wonderful space and resource in school life. At the time of its opening, Eilís placed great emphasis on our school motto, *Ut Sint Unum* ('That they may they be one'). It became a mantra that helped us in happy and sad times, such as celebrating the visit of President Mary McAleese to the school in 2004 and in mourning the untimely loss of our dear colleague, Cathleen Neill, in 2005. In their different ways, both these events showcased what is best about this school. Eilís now works with the Le Chéile Schools Trust, a collaborative trust set up in 2009 by the St Louis Sisters and thirteen other congregations to affirm their commitment to Catholic education and the future of their schools. St Louis High School is one of the sixty second-level schools in the trust.

Having served as deputy principal for two years, Mary Morgan (another dyed-in-the-wool Louis girl) took over the principal's role in 2005. By now the speed of change was dizzying but Mary was more than equal to its demands. It is difficult to believe that such a relatively short time ago, we were all using chalk and blackboards! Now, in addition to our two computer rooms, every classroom is equipped with a data projector and a computer with internet access. The introduction of Moodle (a virtual learning environment) has ensured that teaching and learning can take place well beyond the four walls of the classroom.

Mary is a principal who delights in every aspect of school life, caring for the values of the past as much as the needs of the present. She is an enthusiastic supporter of all extracurricular and co-curricular activities, school tours, workshops and the annual concert and variety show. Along with the staff as a whole and the parent body, she recognises the great contribution to school life and spirit of events like sports day, the school musical and the Young Scientist competition, giving support and encouragement to the teachers who organise them. A significant recent achievement has been the attainment of our third green flag, showing our commitment to a clean and safe environment. Following

St Louis High School staff, 2013-14, with principal Mary Morgan centre-front and deputy principal Geraldine McDonagh on left.
Photo © Robert Allen Photography.

Sixth-year student council members, 2013, from left: Ella Scally, Amy Kiernan, Frances Martin, Katelynn Kavanagh, Caoimhe Bermingham, Kiara Whelan and Katie Barry..
Photo © Robert Allen Photography.

on from the leaders of the past, Mary fosters staff development and school planning, while maintaining a happy school atmosphere, firm but fair discipline and great respect for all members of the school community.

St Louis High School today reminds me of the great poem by W.B. Yeats, 'Among School Children', in which he concludes that we are all the sum of everything we have ever been or experienced.

O chestnut-tree, great-rooted blossomer,
Are you the leaf, the blossom or the bole?
O body swayed to music, O brightening
glance,
How can we know the dancer from the
dance?

Every decade and every individual associated with our school has left an imprint, so that today we have a strong and holistic centre of academic excellence where a broad-based curriculum fosters intellectual, social, artistic, entrepreneurial and spiritual development. We believe that our students are challenged and empowered to become their best selves. We are constantly improving our buildings and facilities, as well as our curriculum and methodologies. New subjects are introduced as we keep pace with developments in society. In our staffroom you will find a blend of youth and experience, ensuring that traditions are passed on and kept safe for coming generations. Louis girls of the past are proud and happy to send us their daughters and we, in our turn, are proud and happy to welcome them to our 'high-class secondary school'.

Kate Hearne

ME AND MY CELLO

Kate Hearne, with her cello and recorder, finds herself settled in Sweden but travels widely to perform and teach the Baroque repertoire.

I am currently living in Sweden, from where I travel widely as a freelance musician. I specialise in Baroque music, playing both the cello and recorder, and perform regularly as a soloist and chamber musician with many different ensembles throughout Europe. After six years at St Louis High School, 1992-1998, I graduated with a BA from the Royal Irish Academy of Music on Westland Row before moving to Sweden to pursue a Masters in Early Music in Stockholm's Royal College of Music.

Despite the cold, dark winters I am still based in Sweden, where musical life is varied and rich. I am now married to a Swedish composer so it looks like I will be here for a while yet! I try to get back to Ireland as often as possible and, as well as giving concerts here, I work as programming and Baroque adviser for the West Cork Chamber Music Festival. I also work as a producer and graphic designer for the concert arrangers Classic Lounge in Malmö. There are very few full-time positions in this field, which means that survival depends on a lot of hard work and the ability to learn many different aspects of the business – not always an easy task!

I have a mission to spread my knowledge to the next generation and although my schedule doesn't permit me to have a regular teaching job, I am involved in many educational projects and give regular master classes and workshops to students at all levels. Three friends from Sweden, Norway and Denmark and I have formed a virtuoso recorder quartet, called Woodpeckers, which travels widely throughout Scandinavia, giving school concerts and workshops. I am also a member of the Baroque Ensemble Concerto Copenhagen, a project-based group of international musicians.

I have received funding for my studies and continuing research from both the Irish and Swedish Arts Councils, the Bank of Ireland Millennium Scholars Trust and Music Network, who have part-funded the many instruments I own, including my Chappuy cello from 1750. In 2005 I won the Montréal International Recorder Competition, which was an incredible experience and helped to launch my career.

My years at St Louis were very happy and I was lucky to meet a bunch of talented and loyal friends, who continue to be an integral part of my life. At St Louis we were encouraged to follow career paths that would be fulfilling and utilise our talents to the best effect. Being good at music and art was never an excuse not to work on academic subjects and I often find myself at an advantage in the music world because we had such a wide and open-minded education. I wouldn't say that St Louis directly influenced my decision to follow a career in music but it certainly helped me to have the maturity to choose wisely and not be afraid to go for a career that seemed a little off the beaten track. So far this year my musical travels have brought me to festivals and interesting concert venues, from north of the Arctic Circle in Norway all the way to the Cervantes Festival in Mexico.

Kate Hearne with a selection of her recorders.

Catherine Loane

'DYING SWANS'

*Catherine Loane wanted to be a ballerina and immersed herself
in Russian culture but found her true métier in the skies
as a captain with Aer Lingus Regional.*

I was very fortunate that St Louis took me in when they did. More than a year earlier, in 1992, I had been in a group of ten lucky girls to attend the Perm Ballet School in Russia. The Soviet Union had collapsed the year before and it seemed a grim place – shops were sparsely stocked, bakeries had queues that stretched around the corner and the rouble was devaluing daily. Basic items such as tea-towels and cutlery still had the price stamped on them, likely unchanged for a decade.

Two of that first group, Katherine O'Malley and I, were asked back for a second year. It was a rare and incredible opportunity but within weeks I knew I had made a mistake. Ballet is a demanding and rigorous profession, particularly the Russian variety, and I realised I enjoyed food too much. Back in Dublin, three

of the girls who had returned to school after one year in Perm – Olwyn, Harriet and Lucy – had changed secondary schools to be together in St Louis. So when Katherine and I returned home for Christmas break, I told my parents I was done with ballet. I wanted to go to St Louis too.

It was now halfway through fifth year and the only classes we had had in the ballet school were Russian and two hours of French a week. In Irish class, I answered in Russian and I was far behind in Maths and Physics. The four of us sat at our own table during lunch, talking Russian. I cringe to recall that I still tied my hair up in a bun and walked with my feet turned out. Our classmates nicknamed us 'the dying swans'. I felt overwhelmed but the patience and perseverance of my teachers ensured that I gradually caught up with the class. It was just in time. My father had taken me on a helicopter ride while on holiday and the drive I had once had for ballet had a new focus – I hoped to become a pilot.

We sat the Leaving Certificate in 1994 and I went on to study Russian and Philosophy in Trinity College. When I could afford it, I took a bus out to Weston Airfield, near Leixlip, for helicopter lessons and ground-school classes, studying for my private pilot's licence. It was a slow process, each lesson costing £200. Aeroplane lessons were half the price, so I changed tack again and was even able to afford to go to America for a month to get my private pilot's licence completed more quickly.

I graduated from TCD and a year later I enrolled in Oxford Aviation College in England. It took sixteen months of hard study and flying lessons to pass ten airline transport pilot exams and a final flight test. Two weeks before I was due to graduate, 9/11 (11 September 2001) brought the aviation industry to its knees. It was a stressful time for all pilots, even those who had been flying for years, as airlines went bust overnight, flight schools closed and the jobs market was awash with eager graduates.

Trying to keep my hand in the business, I took a job with one such doomed airline, EUJet, working shifts in the operations and crewing department. During this time, I sent CVs to airlines all over the world but the months rolled past and as my licences began to expire, it became difficult to remain optimistic. I had just finished a night shift when the phone rang. It was the head of training with Aer Arann, wondering if I was still looking for a flying job and if I could make myself available for interview the following week.

Two months later I was on the line, flying from Dublin to small regional airports in Galway, Sligo and Donegal, which one captain described as like landing on the garden path. Ten years on and Aer Arann is three times the size, with a new fleet of aircraft and a new name – Aer Lingus Regional – operating many of Aer Lingus's short-haul routes around the UK. A captain now, I am delighted that I made the decision to leave ballet and grateful that St Louis provided me with the chance to meet lifelong friends and discover the career path I truly wanted.

Photo by Justin MacInnes.

Mary Finan

THE TIME
OF MY LIFE

*Mary Finan remembers performing in musicals, the thrill of beating the boys
in debating and many good friends from her years in St Louis.*

I queued anxiously in the dark corridor. Sr Clothilde stood at the far end, beside the entrance to the main hall. As each girl approached, she murmured something and the girl entered the hall, moving to the left or right. What was she saying? I drew closer and heard the words 'peasant', 'lady', 'peasant', 'lady' repeated over and over and I realised we were being divided into two groups for the chorus of the operetta. Please God, I prayed, as I checked my nails and smoothed my hair: don't let me be a peasant! The relief I felt when she said 'lady' to me was comparable only to the sensation I experienced on opening my Leaving Certificate results six years later.

It was 1957 and I had arrived in first year in St Louis High School in Rathmines. I had heard about the Christmas operetta. It created a lot of excitement every year and I wanted desperately to be a part of it. This year's production was *The Quaker Girl*. As I could not sing, I had had the good sense not to audition for one of the leading roles but this did not deter me from trying to get into the chorus. And I succeeded, joy of joys! My joy, however, was to be short-lived, because as soon as rehearsals began it became clear to Sr Clothilde that someone was singing out of tune. She stopped and asked each of us to sing a scale. My trembling 'doh, ray…' was sufficient to identify me as the culprit and I was summarily banished.

But all was not lost. Sr Clothilde was kind and some days later asked me to audition for a small speaking part as the mother of the Quaker girl. I got the part and a wonderful old-fashioned riding costume with a long, red skirt and tailored jacket, white stock and a high black hat. Barbara McHugh, tall and slender, was the principal boy and I can still hear the sound of her lovely voice when she came on stage singing:

Ah, Madame, here I am to invite La Quakeress,
May I pray that she'll say as her answer only yes.

Sr Clothilde put me in other choruses, on condition that I 'mouth', but as time went by I began to channel my energy into the worlds of Sr Marie René and Sr Miriam, whose focus on Irish and English debating competitions inspired in us not only a desire to win but an understanding of the importance of developing a well-informed point of view and having the ability to articulate it persuasively. This became an abiding passion for us throughout second level and, thanks to our mentors, we won many awards, including beating the arrogant boys from Synge Street for the Gael Linn Cup, which was a great thrill. Another exciting win was the Hibernia Cup sponsored by Aer Lingus. The prize was a return flight to Cork with Sr Miriam and the team and visits to places of interest around the city – the only one I can remember now is Hadji Bey's, where we consumed vast quantities of the delicious Turkish delight.

For six years St Louis High School was my second home. My two sisters, Gina and Dorothea, were there at the same time. (Gerardine followed later). My friends were there too. Maeve Casley was my best friend. The neatest person on the planet, she ironed her school scarf every day at lunchtime. Her father was a lieutenant colonel in McKee Barracks, where I spent many happy times with her family. Maeve had all the qualities one seeks in a friend: she was loyal, honest, discreet, a trusted confidante. When not visiting Maeve, I would sometimes walk home with Mary Kiely, daughter of Ben, now gone to heaven where she belongs. We would have amiable discussions on anything that took our fancy as we strolled up Rathgar Road. She had her father's talent for conversation and storytelling. At other times, I would join Antoinette O'Reilly and Deirdre O'Grady and go home via Grosvenor Road, carrying our hot-cross buns and billycans of potato soup from domestic science class. Antoinette's father was master tailor to couturier Irene Gilbert and we were all consumed with admiration for her beautiful red-haired mother who wore marvellous outfits to the parents' events. Deirdre loved everything Italian, especially Maria Callas. She told us one day that she had sent a birthday card and a box of chocolates to Callas. Antoinette and I smiled affectionately, but imagine our astonishment and admiration, when, a few weeks later, Deirdre produced a thank-you letter from the great diva.

My class was full of lovable and talented people. Dara de Brí was quiet and looked like a Botticelli muse. One day a photographer came to the school searching for a girl to appear on the cover of a religious magazine and chose Dara. None of us was surprised. Helena Dempsey was a ballerina and always had us giggling whenever a teacher left the room. One day she told a story about her father, who was a man of habit. He always parked his car outside the front door and washed it every Saturday morning. The preceding Saturday, however, he had mistakenly washed the next-door neighbour's car because her mother had taken theirs to go shopping. He did not realise it until the neighbour called to thank him. Pat Moran was a woman of the world. She had tasted vodka and had a boyfriend. I envied her and imagined him as a Cossack on a white horse. Emer Forde was womanly too but in a different way. She always behaved in an adult fashion and seemed to have an understanding of life that escaped me. She was the one I would go to for practical advice.

St Louis was a benign environment where we were encouraged to pursue our own interests and realise our potential in the process. They were simpler times. It is true we were more easily entertained then but we were also engaged and most of us derived enormous satisfaction from school life. I can honestly say that I believe youth was not wasted on the class of 1963. I benefitted greatly from the ethos that prevailed in St Louis during those years and trust it still endures. Our teachers understood that education is far broader than a classroom curriculum and opened our minds to what was going on in the world around us. Most of them were nuns who were happy to devote all the time it took, over evenings and weekends, to help us achieve our best in the fields of music, debating and sport, as well as in academic subjects. They built a sense of a community where we looked out for one another. They equipped us to occupy a place in the world and lead a decent life. Above all, they taught us the importance of repaying the gifts we were given and for this I will be forever grateful.

Siobhán Supple

THE OPEN DOOR

The Sisters of St Louis originated in France, just one of the many European countries with which exchanges of pupils and teachers were organised.

Bearing in mind that the Sisters of St Louis founded the congregation's first school in Juilly, near Paris, in 1842, after which the order established itself in Ireland, with schools in Monaghan (1859), Carrickmacross (1899), Kiltimagh (1907) and Rathmines (1913), it is no surprise that wide horizons and international communications and programmes have played a significant role in St Louis High School. Pupil and teacher exchanges and participation in European projects were fostered, the initiatives supported enthusiastically by the whole school community.

Sr Kathleen O'Sullivan set up an exchange programme with France in 1975, at first with Malmaison and subsequently with the St Louis school in Juilly, Cours Bautain. The two-week visit was open to second-year students, accompanied by teachers. Students were accommodated in host families. They attended normal classes with their partners, as well as special language classes, and enjoyed cultural visits and outings from Juilly and Rathmines. This exchange prospered and continued for many years until circumstances changed in Juilly. The last exchange was in 2004.

St Louis schools have always strongly supported the teaching of German and exchanges were offered from 1974 onwards. Exchange locations included Köln, Frankfurt, Freiburg im Breisgau, Pfaffenhoffen in Bavaria and Bad Salzungen in Thuringia. The longest-running exchange was with the Realschule in Pfaffenhoffen, which ran from 1991 until 2009.

Though exchange programmes do not directly include all students, the benefit to the school community is well worth the effort they require.

For those who participate there is an increased recognition of the value of acquiring a foreign language. An exchange offers the experience of living in a family abroad; learning new customs and ways of looking at life; dealing with new sounds, smells, tastes and homesickness. These tasks are not always easy for thirteen- or fourteen-year-olds but the experience encourages independence and tolerance and opens new horizons.

The inclusive philosophy of St Louis reached even into individual exchange programmes. As visiting pupils attended classes they were distributed throughout the year group and not always with the exchange partner, thereby facilitating more contact between the host and visiting pupils. An exchange opens the door to other cultures, helps students to develop self-awareness and a sense of identity and paves the way for further contacts and adventures.

Always to the forefront, St Louis embraced each new challenge and, when teacher exchanges were offered, Brídín Gilroy, Sharon Muldoon, Ann Taylor, Sinéad Ní Fhlanagáin and Siobhán Supple grasped the opportunity. Further exchanges and European programmes grew out of these contacts with Avignon (Monique Vincent, 1985); Valladolid (Pilar Salamanca, 1990); Athens (Maria Kalogirou, 1995); Frankfurt; Pfaffenhoffen (Peter Krauss, 1991); Bad Salzungen; Helsinki and Kenni, Finland

(Kaarina Linstorm, 1998); Copenhagen; Belgium; Luxembourg; and Strasbourg. These new contacts blossomed into participation in the Young Linguists' Competition (1986), Comenius programmes, multilateral school partnerships and Euroscola visits to the EU parliament in Strasbourg, among others experiences.

Many schools in France and Germany are co-educational, something that added an extra dimension of planning to exchange visits, resulting in partnerships with St Mary's College, Rathmines, as well as other girls' schools, such as Our Lady's, Templeogue, and Sancta Maria, Ballyroan, if extra numbers were required.

Though exchanges cause much disruption to normal school life, fellow staff members were always supportive. Over the years it was not only language teachers who ventured off on exchange visits or European programmes with pupils from St Louis: all departments were represented in escorting, supervising or actively participating in study programmes.

In 1990-1 an Irish arts' week, with joint Irish and Spanish funding, formed part of the exchange that Brídín Gilroy arranged with Valladolid. Irish artists performed and a plaque to Red Hugh O'Donnell, who came to Spain for help after the Battle of Kinsale in the early 17th century, was erected in the city.

Arising directly from teacher exchanges with Avignon and Valladolid, a multilateral school project with visits was sanctioned, funded by the EU. The project, which ran from 1992 to 1994, was an investigation of river quality and use, drawing comparisons between the Rhône, the Pisuerga and the Dodder! Teachers and students from the science, geography and language departments were involved. They made study visits to Avignon and Valladolid and published their findings, which were presented in St Louis High School.

Encouraged by this success in multilateral research, the school embarked on another Comenius programme in 1996. This time we linked up with Denmark, Avignon and Bad Salzungen to investigate social and cultural change between 1950 and 1990, under the title *The Times They Are a-Changing*. Certainly a changing world, as we visited closed mines in Bad Salzungen and looked at work patterns in our own country and those of partners, as well as family life, urban development and cuisine. We all finally met up together at the European Parliament Euroscola in Strasbourg in 1997. A party of thirty, comprising students and teachers from all the St Louis schools in Ireland, made their way to Strasbourg, travelling via Paris, Juilly, where the St Louis Institute was founded and Turkenstein, Alsace, the spiritual home of the Institute. We had proud moments as some of our party were chosen to address the whole

Euroscola assembly in the parliament building in Strasbourg.

A further pupil exchange to Bad Salzungen took place in June 1998. Other programmes followed and regular language exchanges continued, each strand feeding into and supporting the others. Some lucky transition-year students benefitted from an exchange programme with Girton Grammar, Bendigo, Australia, a co-educational school. A history project took students to Helsinki in 1996, fifth-year students carried out a prizewinning pure water study in Belgium in 1996 and there was a study trip to Denmark in 1997.

St Louis Rathmines warmly welcomed the concept of cultural diversity, which was celebrated with a world languages' day in 2001 and an international club set up by pupils Maedhbh Halpenny and Isabelle Zang in 2005, which embraced the richness of difference.

St Louis European studies cross-border project continued the trend by winning the flyer design competition for all-expenses-paid visits to Euroscola in both 2010 and 2011.

Now the focus has moved to Kano, Nigeria, where one of the first St Louis schools in Africa was founded in 1948. Teacher exchanges took place in 2010 and 2011, facilitated by the work of TY classes under the direction of

Barbara Capper, and it is hoped that in time this will lead to further contacts and exchanges. Horizons grow wider, the world grows smaller and St Louis certainly lives up to its motto, *Ut Sint Unum* ('That they may they be one').

I have always been passionate about exchanges and contact with other countries, languages and people and started sending my own children abroad from the age of ten. At first they complained, sulked, scowled and even wept but they grew to appreciate the experience and are now doing the same with their own children. Without a doubt, exchange visits, whether pupil- or teacher-based, push open the door to the wider world and encourage growth, enthusiasm, healthy curiosity and a perception of otherness, thereby increasing awareness of one's own identity.

Students from all the St Louis schools on a 1997 Euroscola visit to the European Parliament in Strasbourg.

Betty Foley

AN INNOVATOR WITH VISION

Betty Foley remembers her colleague Eibhlín Breathnach: feminist, radical and totally engagée *history teacher who helped the winds of change blow in St Louis.*

Eibhlín Breathnach came to St Louis High School Rathmines in 1969, two years before I did. It was, apart from her Higher Diploma year in Sion Hill in Blackrock, her first job.

To understand the impact she made on the school it is important to remember that Eibhlín came from an Ireland that was very different from that of today. It was a country where in religion one was either Catholic or Protestant – atheists were the few exceptions out there on the margins and to be wondered at – and ecumenism had never been heard of. Although Vatican II had happened it had little impact on a Church or a people who were very conservative and rigidly Catholic. Most of the schools were run by priests, nuns and brothers with a strong faith ethic. Ireland was trying to reclaim its cultural heritage in music and dance and desperate attempts were being made to revive the Irish language. We were still living in the aftermath of the Civil War and we did not join the EU until 1973. Economically we were a poor agricultural country that relied on the UK almost totally for exports. Emigration to England and America was the norm and very different from what it is today: when one went it was unlikely that one would ever return and the misery of American wakes were close to the Irish consciousness. Frugality and austerity were the order of the day, even though now we tend to think that we have the monopoly on austerity!

Free secondary education had arrived in Ireland only two years before Eibhlín came to Rathmines. Social norms were very rigid; feminism was very new and probably a sin; in general men were the breadwinners and women minded the homes. Divorce, contraception and gay rights were unheard of and children born out of wedlock were labelled illegitimate.

There was one television station in Ireland which was established in Eibhlín's teens and one radio station and both were heavily censored. The BBC could be accessed only on the east coast, through a cloud of snow, and in the border counties. Computers were something akin to science fiction.

Politically there were Fianna Fáil and Fine Gael, continuing civil war politics, with the Labour Party hovering somewhere on the edge, and communism was a sin. Sport meant the GAA. There had been a ban on playing foreign games and even when the ban was lifted many people disapproved of those who became involved in soccer or rugby.

In his Nobel Prize acceptance speech in 1995, Seamus Heaney – only a few years older than Eibhlín – described the Ireland in which he grew up: 'We lived in a kind of den-like existence, which was more or less emotionally and intellectually proofed against the outside world; ahistorical, pre-sexual, in suspension between the archaic and the modern, we were as susceptible and impressionable as the drinking water that stood in a bucket in our scullery.'

Such was the Ireland of Eibhlín's childhood. While she was in her later years in school and certainly when she went to UCD to do her degree in history the winds of change were beginning to blow. Beatlemania swept the country, the hippie movement had begun. Contraceptives brought a measure of sexual freedom, although they were not legal in Ireland until 1973, so had to be purchased across the border or on trips to London. There was a gradual opening out towards the modern world. Censorship of books eased and then disappeared and a growing liberalism permeated this 'den-like' existence.

There are two possible reactions to any great shift in consciousness: to become entrenched and hostile to change; or to react with openness and excitement; to be willing to be changed by the rightness of new thinking; to become discerning and inclusive by attempting to bring this new consciousness into one's life and work. The latter was the reaction that Eibhlín embraced with a passion. She was by nature curious and radical; she was not hostile to change but willing to incorporate the excitement and freshness of the new with the best of the old.

The impact this had on her twenty years in St Louis High School is very interesting. Many of the democratic principles that operate in the school today and are so taken for granted by staff and students came about because she was open to change and because, in the 1970s and 1980s, she worked in cooperation with some enormously progressive and enlightened staff members and with Anne Murray SSL, a wonderful principal who shared her love of history and had a similar free and radical way of thinking and who believed in 'devolved' government rather than hierarchical authority. So Eibhlín had the freedom to think and implement new ideas.

One of my memories of Eibhlín is of her incredible enthusiasm. When referenda and general elections were held in the country, she set up polling stations in the library for the school community, staff and students. Members of her history classes were the candidates, the returning officers and the tally women. They counted the votes and, as returning officers, announced the results. The abortion referendum of 1983, which was carried in the country, was defeated in St Louis, something that made the pages of *The Irish Times*.

Eibhlín was responsible for setting up the student representative council and was its coordinator for many years. She passionately believed in democracy and the organisation was run on strict democratic principles. She promoted the views, opinions and requests of students without flinching, at times having to take an unpopular stance on their behalf. A devoted trade unionist, she served as the ASTI shop steward – something that brought her into conflict with management at times. She was not shy in expressing her views publicly and privately but she always did so with respect. In the spirit of a true liberal, she could hear another point of view and even understand it, although it might have been totally at variance with her own. More than anything else, I learned from her the value of this openness.

Eibhlín was a great feminist, very committed to the cause: her MA thesis was entitled *Women in Higher Education in the 19th Century in Ireland*. She communicated this commitment to the students and loved debating issues concerning feminism. Though liberal in outlook, she never lost her interest in the Catholic Church and was as curious and interested in matters concerning faith as she was in other areas.

Eibhlín loved Ireland and her favourite era in Irish history was the mediaeval period. My friend, Bernadette Mullan, remembers her building mediaeval castles for her children on the beach in Bettystown. She wrote a textbook on mediaeval history that was used in schools for many years and my memory of her is moving from classroom to classroom with model castles and monasteries which often fell apart, as well as endless bits of paper and notes of interest that she picked up from various sources. This was the pre-computer age: we had a contraption called a Gestetner which was messy and unreliable – a forerunner of the modern copier. She did most of her work in longhand. I remember that at one stage she learned to type and when she revived the school magazine she typed every word of all the articles herself. Eibhlín was a European and nothing gave her greater pleasure than travelling to Europe and when possible organising school trips to European countries.

Recently I attended a school reunion of the class of 1986. Many of the past pupils had not heard of Eibhlín's sudden and untimely death in 2005 and I was very struck by how sad and upset they were. Their memories were of an inspiring teacher and how she used to encourage and empower them to write letters regarding human rights abuses when she set up Amnesty International in the school.

Writing this piece about Eibhlín, I want to communicate a person who was alive, curious, interested, respectful, kind, funny and tremendously interesting. This was the impact she had on the school community, this is her legacy and those of us who worked with her remember her as a wonderful friend, a valued colleague and a superb teacher whose mark is on the school – and a good mark it is!

Eibhlín Breathnach.

Musical trio, from left: Gráinne Gormley, Ella Adler and Ursula Hough.

Ursula Hough, Gráinne Gormley, Ella Adler

THREE GENERATIONS IN ST LOUIS

*Daughter, mother and grandmother remember schooldays
in which music played a major part.*

URSULA HOUGH

I arrived for my first day in St Louis Rathmines in September 1944. I was four and was joining Sr Gemma's babies class in St Louis Hall which was at the end of the hill when you entered the big gates on Charleville Road. I adored it. There were small music rooms off the porch where I started the violin with Sr Helena and later piano with Sr Clothilde.

On the lawn to the side of the hall there was a maypole. We had drill and dancing with Mrs Redmond and on summer days we danced most intricate routines with beautifully coloured ribbons around the maypole.

After high babies and First Holy Communion class, I moved up to Wakefield House to Sr Geneviève and from then to 6th class was in Wynnefield House. During these seven years plans were afoot for the building of the new school and Assumpta Hall. Assumpta Hall opened with an operetta, *Princess Chrysanthemum*, which was set in Japan. I played the part of Topknot, the princess's chamberlain. My first line announced her arrival, so at the top of my voice I said, 'The Princess and her suite have arrived.' I thought the suite referred to was a suite of furniture and was convinced of this for years.

From the first day I entered St Louis there were concerts, operettas, choirs, orchestras, pageants, Feis Ceoil competitions and trips to St Louis Monaghan to see their shows, as well as piano, violin, cello, viola and singing lessons. I was the second eldest of eight and we all went to St Louis: the two boys, Kevin and Michael, just as far as Holy Communion class. The six girls were in all the operettas, which were directed by the renowned producer, Eileen Knowles. On the final night of one particular production of *The Student Prince*, John Larchet, Professor of Music in UCD, spoke from the stage and suggested that the production go to the Gaiety Theatre. The cast in the operetta that year included Hazel Yeomans and Betty Ann Norton.

For all our choral competitions in the Feis Ceoil, the colourful Terry O'Connor was our conductor. Sr Clothilde was our choral mistress but because she was a nun she could not conduct in public, so Terry came in for the last week of rehearsal and Kitty O'Callaghan joined her as our accompanist. These ladies were two of the biggest names in the Irish music scene at the time – only the best for St Louis! The worst thing about these rehearsals was that at the break, nuns came into the hall carrying trays with tea and wonderful things to eat for the two ladies, while we stood and watched with our tongues hanging out with hunger as rehearsals were after school and it was by then

about five in the evening. On the day of the Feis we all had to line up at the door before we left for the Metropolitan Hall in Abbey Street and swallow some dreadful stuff from a spoon, which Sr Clothilde told us was good for our voices. Funnily enough, we always won! The Royal Irish Academy choir and orchestra exams were another big annual event and our plainchant choir participated in these.

As each of us left St Louis, we joined the St Louis past pupils' union and St Louis musical society. We felt indebted to the founders of these organisations and I find it very sad that they are no longer in existence. St Louis musical society made history by winning the Waterford International Festival of Light Opera three years in succession and taking two of the winning shows, *The Boyfriend* and *The Golden Years,* to the Gaiety and Olympia Theatres respectively on our return. We appeared on *The Late Late Show* after we had won in Waterford with *The Golden Years* and our eleven trophies were on display in the studio. The sparkle of the Waterford Glass trophies under the strong lights of Studio One was a sight to behold. Alas, the Waterford Festival too is no more.

The day I left St Louis I cried with sadness. I loved every day I was there. My school pals are still my dearest pals and our little gang meets regularly although, unfortunately, one or two have gone to their reward. My career as a professional violinist started in 1944 in the little music room in St Louis Hall with Sr Helena and Sr Clothilde and I will always be grateful to them and to the other Sisters and lay teachers of the school for all they did for us.

GRÁINNE GORMLEY

I could begin on the day I became a St Louis pupil, my first day – September 1974 – and my first classroom, Room 16, a prefabricated structure of sagging floors and limited heat, a damp and windswept distance from the warmth and solidity of the main building. Or I could go back even further, to my first visit to Charleville Road: a production of Oklahoma by the past pupils' musical society, my father playing the role of Jud Fry and me, aged three, inconsolable when he is 'killed' in the final scene, then wonderfully reassured in his arms after the final curtain, the smell of greasepaint and floor polish anchoring me once again in comfort and connection.

This early memory and my arrival at the school gates in 1974 bookend what was, in fact, a childhood colonised by the personalities and experiences that shaped my mother's time in St Louis: Sr Fulgentia, Sr Clothilde – such exotic names – plays, feiseanna and musicals; Latin and long lunch breaks, as well as by my teenage aunts, glamorous harbingers in shades of wine and cream of my future scholastic life in Rathmines. For there was no doubt that

I would follow my mother and aunts and become a Louis girl. While this inevitability might have created a feeling of pressure, a sense that there was a 'Hough standard' that I would have to maintain, my memories are of happy anticipation, curiosity, wondering what it would be like to sit in the classrooms where they had studied, stand on the stage where they had sung.

And so it began, my five-year secondary education in St Louis, There are many aspects of this experience that I could recall and explore here: my introduction to a body of knowledge through the expert and encouraging guidance of the Sisters and lay staff; the teachers who made a significant impact by virtue of their skill in communicating their passion for their subjects, in particular my teachers of English and Irish: Ita Daly, Pauline Slattery, Lily O'Donovan and Sr Mairéad Hughes; and my fellow Louis girls – the fun, mischief, challenge and support we generated among ourselves.

I was especially fortunate to be part of Room 9 in sixth year, a room which became the stuff of legend in the years following our graduation, thanks to the extraordinary dynamic within our class and our achievements in our final year, when we were winners in the drama festival, the choral competition and – our proudest moment – the tidy classroom competition! We were involved in every aspect of school life, our contributions shaped by a cohesiveness and loyalty that were really quite special.

However, as with my mother and aunts, it was my musical education in St Louis that had the greatest impact on my life, shaping my intellectual and emotional development, informing many important decisions and continuing to contribute in a meaningful way to my personal and professional life. Sr Joan Morris guided and supported me through the Intermediate and Leaving Certificate syllabi with patience and skill and I will forever be grateful to her for promoting good aural skills and a solid grounding in basic music theory as essential elements of a musical education. I continue, to this day, to automatically translate everything I hear into tonic solfa!

Then there was my introduction to choral singing, through the exceptional skills of Iris Maguire, who had the ability to tame hundreds of restless teenage girls by her unique blend of humour, firmness and astonishing musicianship, coaxing the most miraculous sounds out of normally recalcitrant adolescents. I learned so much about singing, communication and repertoire during our weekly choral sessions.

Perhaps Iris's greatest gift to me was her idea of creating an inter-class choral competition. Classes from each year group would compete, the best choir from each year then meeting in a final round to determine the overall winner. The first competition took place when I was in fourth year. We chose a piece of music from a list set by Iris. Then came another decision: who would conduct the class? Someone suggested I do it as I was, at that stage, studying singing and piano at the College of Music. I can still remember the moment when I walked to the top of the class and looked down at the serried ranks of my fellow pupils, their faces raised expectantly towards me. I remember feeling calm, feeling a 'rightness' about what I was about to do. I raised my hands. I looked out into the room, raised my right hand a little higher and, as one, the class began to sing.

Having struggled with a stammer since childhood, I felt the joy of being able to communicate non-verbally, to create sound through the medium of my hands, body and face. For three years, I conducted my class in the choral competition, my skill and confidence growing, and we won the overall competition in sixth year, a moment of great pride for us all. I went on to do a BMus degree in UCD and a master's degree in choral conducting in the University of North Carolina, followed by a decade of teaching and conducting in colleges and communities in Dublin.

For the past twenty years I have conducted the choir of St Teresa's, Clarendon Street. I feel immensely fortunate to be part of a community in which the canon of Church music, spanning a millennium of compositional endeavour, is valued and integrated into every liturgy. I am grateful to have that space in which to channel my musical spirit. And I continue to be so grateful for that moment in fourth year when something special was awakened within me.

I stand on the gallery in St Teresa's, I raise my hands, I look out, raise my right hand a little higher and, as one, the members of the choir, begin to sing…

ELLA ADLER

My favourite day of the St Louis calendar was the annual open day, on which we opened our doors to prospective Louis girls and prospective Louis parents. I think we enjoyed it because our school was such an easy sell. Naturally we took great pains to ensure it was looking its best. There was a carefully crafted chain of students and teachers to welcome our visitors and the poster-making began weeks in advance. But really we need not have bothered. St Louis always had an incredible atmosphere. Enthusiasm was the norm, even on Mondays. Our welcome on the open day was in no way manufactured or false; it was the same welcome that would be given any day of the week.

Perhaps this constant warm atmosphere stemmed from the immense pride we all had in our school and in one another. When I was in fifth year a few of us attended a ceremony in Trinity College to receive our silver Gaisce awards. My abiding memory of the evening is that the keynote speaker singled us out as a group and praised our enthusiasm. I guess he picked up on the wild cheers every time one of us was mentioned. The pride was reinforced by the knowledge that around each student was a strong network of support. I have such an appreciation for the personal approach of the teachers. Someone would always notice if something was not quite right, if the mood in a class was not what it should be, if someone needed extra help.

It seems that school pride was just as strong in my grandmother's time. It was always a little hard to imagine that she and my mother traipsed the same halls as I did. There's a photograph in one of the corridors of the entire school in 1958 or so. Every once in a while I would stop and stare at it. I figured I was related to at least one girl in the picture but could never make it out.

I was lucky enough to be head girl in 2009-2010. I liked to see my role as caretaker of the school spirit, the school's greatest asset. My old, slightly battered head-girl badge was a tangible artefact of the history of St Louis. To have that in my possession for a year, knowing that it was worn just as proudly in my grandmother's time and in my mother's time, was really very special.

Photo by Luca Truffarelli.

Katherine O'Malley

A PASSION FOR DANCE

Katherine O'Malley recalls a life spent in dance,
ballet and later contemporary.

I spent only two years in St Louis High School but I remember them fondly. They were my last two years in a conventional school before I left for Russia. Between arriving at the start of third year and leaving after transition year I made lifelong friends in St Louis and I received wonderful support from the staff as it grew increasingly obvious that I was to choose an unusual path. In particular, I had a connection with Sr Gemma Gibbons, as her sister had married into my father's family. She was retired but had been a music teacher with St Louis Primary School and had a great appreciation of the arts. She was a huge support to me as I was planning to make a life-changing decision.

St Louis was very close to the Dublin School of Classical and Contemporary Dance in Portobello, where I spent most evenings after school, along with Harriet Parsons, another St Louis student and a close friend to this day. When I reached the age of fifteen and dance gradually took precedence over schoolwork, the staff in St Louis gave me great guidance and, like my parents, ultimately listened to what it was I wanted for myself.

During fourth year I auditioned to train in the Vaganova Ballet Academy summer school in St Petersburg and also in its sister school in Siberia, the Perm State Choreographic School. I was accepted to the summer school but the audition for Perm was more rigorous and I was

119

not accepted for full-time training immediately. In July 1991 I travelled to St Petersburg. My education at the Vaganova Academy was an incredible experience and I knew I wanted to stay. I remember receiving a telegram from my parents on my sixteenth birthday and realising how far from home I had travelled.

Only a couple of weeks after my return from St Petersburg, I was accepted at Perm, just after an attempted coup was thwarted in Moscow. Unsurprisingly, given the political climate in Russia, family members had mixed feelings about my going to live there. I remember seeing the photograph of Boris Yeltsin on a tank and wondering what I would be getting myself into. After much soul-searching and discussion with my parents, I set off to Perm via Moscow and the Transiberian Railway. I was delighted. Perm was a closed city before 1991 and myself, Lucy Hickey, Catherine Loane, Olwyn Leo and Harriet Parsons, four St Louis alumnae, as well as four other Irish girls, were some of the very few westerners who visited that year.

After two years I received an honours graduate diploma under the tutorship of the artistic director, Ludmila Pavlovna Sakharova. In 1994, I joined the corps de ballet of the Tatar State Opera and Ballet Theatre, Kazan. I toured throughout Europe, visiting Germany, Holland, France and Ireland with ballet and opera productions including *Swan Lake*, Giselle, *Sleeping Beauty*, *The Nutcracker Suite*, *La Bayadère*, *Don Quixote*, *Prince Igor*, *The Flying Dutchman*, *Ivan the Terrible* and *La Traviata*.

I changed focus in 1998 and undertook a further year of training in London Contemporary Dance School. On my return to Dublin I became a founding member of Rex Levitates Dance Company, now known as the Liz Roche Company, and in 2008 I became associate dance artist. As a performer and associate artist I assist company artistic director and choreographer, Liz Roche, on various projects, residencies, festivals and commissions in Ireland, Northern Ireland, UK, China, Germany, France, Spain and USA. As a freelance artist I have worked in dance, theatre and opera in Europe, Asia, Australia and North America.

I recently completed my Masters Degree in Contemporary Dance Performance in the University of Limerick, where I currently teach contemporary dance to postgraduate students. I hope I can support my students, as I was supported at St Louis, to demonstrate and realise their gifts and help them to find possibilities in a range of career options.

Fionnuala Parfrey

DOORS ON WHICH I NEVER KNOCKED

Fionnuala Parfrey acknowledges the influence of her teachers of French and chemistry and an open-minded school that encouraged her to 'try everything'.

Even though I'm living in Paris I knew my mother, Jo O'Donoghue, was involved in publishing this centenary book. Jo rightly assumed that it wouldn't interest me to sentimentalise my high school years but having read the proofs of this book – an extra pair of eyes – I didn't find sentimentality to be the prevailing mood. Most of the accounts are more concerned with the present than with eulogising the past. The more I read the more I wanted to try to relate my present situation to my time in St Louis.

I have a strong sense that I was given every opportunity to pursue a varied and individuated education when I was in St Louis. Initially I was unhappy with the final subject options for the senior cycle. I had wanted to give up on the natural sciences entirely and take an arts-centred Leaving Certificate, with history, French, music and art supplementing my three obligatory subjects. But history and music clashed on the timetable, which led me to do music outside school and take up chemistry – in which I had no earthly interest. Ms Hanrahan saved me, though. Somehow the subject clicked when she taught it, so much so that I even considered it as an option for third level! Chemistry gave me an A1 and was quite possibly the reason I got my place in Trinity.

Something about that experience helped me to realise the value of keeping an open mind and being able to look at life from a variety of perspectives. When I look back at St Louis I feel that every little bit fell into place in the end and this was quite possibly the result of a certain spirit of open-mindedness and acceptance in the school.

At the moment I am doing a masters in visual culture in Paris, French being the other great love instilled in me at school. Ms Carragher and the French debating team have a lot to answer for (and how stressful speaking French in public was for me at the time). While I almost chose to study French and English in Trinity I couldn't be more glad that I didn't. My choice of film studies and the visual arts has led me down an exciting route and into an academic field about which I feel very passionate. Yet I am back in France for a second year, having done an Erasmus while an undergraduate, and have had the opportunity to master the language at my own pace.

As I progressed through St Louis, all doors remained open to me, including ones on which I had never knocked, and this has led me to look at life as a series of exciting and unpredictable opportunities. I think the diversity of the curriculum at St Louis and the encouragement given to the students to try everything and explore all their potential talents are among the school's strongest points. I don't really know what is ahead of me career-wise but I am grateful that St Louis encouraged me to pursue my passions and have faith in the unknown.

Fionnuala Parfrey in Front Square, TCD. Photo by Marion Jousseaume.

Paula McNamee

SPORTS IN ST LOUIS

PE teacher Paula McNamee surveys sporting activities and adventures in St Louis High School, for the 21st century and beyond.

Sport in St Louis High School, Rathmines continues to grow and develop into the 21st century, both through the channels of the PE programme taught by Paula McNamee, Aoife Rogers and Darren O'Meara and the broad range of extracurricular activities organised by our sports coordinator, Darina Halpenny.

For the PE curriculum, students cover seven strands in the junior cycle, which include athletics, aquatics, dance, games, gymnastics, health-related fitness and outdoor adventure education. In the senior cycle, the main emphasis is on health-related fitness programmes, as well as the more traditional curriculum of games, athletics and outdoor adventure.

While we continue to await the promised building of a new gym facility for the school, the opening in 2010 of the Swan Leisure Centre in Rathmines (ten minutes' walk from school) has enhanced the quality of the PE programme at both junior and senior level.

The PE department organises many extra-curricular trips, including local trips to the Spawell pitch 'n' putt centre in Templeogue. On a regional level, second-year students go for a one-day outdoor education programme in Baltinglass, County Wicklow. On a national level, TY students take a five-day outdoor education programme at the Petersburg Outdoor Education Centre in Clonbur, County Galway. On an international level

Above: Sal Austin White (TY) comes down the rapids at Petersburg Outdoor Education Centre, 2012.

Below: Lauren Delaney (left) and Aoife Burke (TY) at Petersburg Outdoor Education Centre, 2012.

we organise a biennial week-long ski trip to a European resort, usually in Austria or Italy.

At cross-curricular level, we cooperate with the science and home economics departments to enhance our health-related fitness programmes. Our sports day, held in May each year, continues to delight participants, students and staff alike, competitive and otherwise.

In terms of sport, St Louis continues to enjoy success at local and national level across the various disciplines.

BASKETBALL

St Louis had a highly successful basketball club under the expert coaching of PE teacher, Helena Murphy, in the 1980s. The club has undergone many changes since then and has re-emerged as a formidable outfit under the guidance of our coach Ciaran Dunne. The minor, junior cadet and senior teams bring home much-prized silverware on a seasonal basis.

VOLLEYBALL

Volleyball emerged as a sport in the 1990s, coached by PE teacher, Paula McNamee. The club has enjoyed much success both at junior and at senior level, culminating in a place in the All-Ireland final of 1998, when Naoise Byrne was captain.

HOCKEY

Hockey has enjoyed considerable success over the years. At first PE teacher Aoife Rogers coached the team; today the students play in the schools' league and train in the Iveagh Grounds under the expert eye of Irish international player and past pupil, Niamh Small.

SWIMMING

The swimming club has brought glory to the school down through the years under the combined guidance of Pauline Holt (PE teacher) and Darina Halpenny (sports coordinator). At local level, the school has enjoyed success in the Dublin Corporation swimming gala, returning the trophy to the school on an annual basis.

The club's champion swimmers have enjoyed success at provincial, national and international level, most notably past pupil Aisling Cooney, who represented Ireland in the Beijing Olympics in 2008.

Many of our swimmers have moved into water safety, coached by Paul Murphy and Darina Halpenny, and over the past ten years we have built up a very successful water-safety club. Students compete at inter-county level and have also added to the school's silverware.

ATHLETICS CLUB

The athletics club continues to flourish under the leadership of Eamon Brennan and coach

Philip Halpin. The girls compete at local, provincial and national level and have brought a good deal of silverware to the school trophy cabinet.

GAELIC FOOTBALL

With the arrival of our new PE teacher, Darren O'Meara, there was a renaissance of interest in Gaelic football. The pupils entered the Dublin League this year and are on course for competitive success.

BADMINTON

Our badminton club has enjoyed success over the years, bringing back silverware in the Leinster Schools Championship. The club has grown and is flourishing under the guidance of our coach Sian Williams. Members will compete in the school leagues in September 2014.

RUGBY

As a result of the achievement of the Irish women's rugby team, St Louis 'answered the call' and in a short span of six months our rugby team has achieved great success. Two students have been selected to play at Leinster interprovincial level, and our juniors are making great headway.

TABLE TENNIS CLUB

Table tennis continues to be enjoyed at a recreational level under the expert guidance of our coach Gerry Dignam. A competitive aspect may be introduced in the near future.

We pride ourselves in the success of sport at St Louis High School and we look forward, in this our centenary year, to continued enjoyment and achievement both on and off the field.

Sibéal Carolan

BASKETBALL IN ST LOUIS

*Sibéal Carolan looks back on almost half a century of basketball
in St Louis High School, recalling some notable successes
as well as the general benefits of the sport.*

When Sr Máire Muldowney asked me to write a piece about basketball for the St Louis High School centenary book I could only say yes, as memories of my happy years in St Louis came rushing back. This reflection will refer to the development of basketball in Ireland and basketball teams in St Louis, linking the game with attributes that live on beyond our school years and make a significant difference to our lives.

Most people mistakenly think that basketball is a relatively new sport in Ireland, an American import, but, in fact, basketball has been played in Ireland since the early 1920s, when Sergeant Major Doogan first introduced the sport into the army. Initially it was regarded as an auxiliary gymnasium exercise for boxers in training but before long it gained the status of a game in its own right. Basketball has remained popular in the army ever since. It then began to grow in popularity outside the army and, in March 1945, the first club was formed in UCD, the first intervarsity competition being held the following year.

The Amateur Basketball Association of Ireland (ABAI) was also formed in 1945. In 1947, the first area board, the Dublin County Board, was set up and the following year the first Leinster championships were held. Irish basketball affiliated with FIBA (Fédération Internationale

de Basket-ball) in 1947 and basketball became firmly established as a recognised sport in this country.

A year later, in 1948, Ireland sent a basketball team to the Olympics held in Britain, a country still recovering from the effects of the Second World War. There was no qualification system for participating teams and this was the only time in the history of the sport that Ireland had a representative team at the Olympics. When Irish basketball celebrated its fiftieth anniversary in 1997, members of the 1948 Olympic squad were present at a reception in the National Basketball Arena in Dublin to honour the founding members of Irish basketball. The first men's national basketball leagues were introduced in 1971-2 and the women's national leagues began in the 1979-80 season.

Basketball Ireland (BI) is the national governing body for the sport in Ireland, with responsibility for the promotion, development and administration of all basketball activities throughout the island. Its primary aim is to increase participation levels in basketball and to provide professionally managed courses, competitions, leagues and services to the basketball public. The board of Basketball Ireland, which comprises voluntary members, governs overall policy. Basketball is the second most popular physical activity among the twelve-eighteen age group, after soccer.

In preparation for writing this piece, I reviewed St Louis yearbooks and had discussions with past pupils Marguerite James and Miriam Breen. They generated lots of interesting information and highlighted the importance of keeping good archives. For many decades St Louis was renowned for its achievements in basketball. In the school basketball was available to all students and teams were formed in three categories: juniors, cadets and seniors. Teams took part in several school leagues with good results, while many players secured places on national teams. For instance, in 1982, Jeanne Moriarty and Jean Ryan secured places in the Dublin under-seventeen and under-fifteen teams respectively and Jeanne was later selected for the national team.

Above: The first basketball team in St Louis High School, 1965.
Front row, from left: Mary Brady, Brenda McCarthy, Frances McCarthy, Peggy Wakefield.
Back row, from left: Sheila O'Byrne, Clare Rankin, Philomena O'Beirne, Rita Daly, Anne Murphy.

Below: The St Louis Senior basketball team that won the All-Ireland final in March 1977,
defeating Manor House School, Raheny, by twelve points.
Front row, from left: Eileen Casey, Marguerite McGovern, Mary McGovern.
Back row, from left: Ann Heffernan, Mary O'Driscoll, Veronica Hopkins.

The commitment St Louis has shown to basketball and other sports demonstrates its commitment to a rounded curriculum, balancing academic achievements with life skills that can be transferred to many other settings. Students and teachers were fully engaged with the sport, so that there was a real partnership approach. A few of the many who promoted basketball in the school were Don McKenna and his son Patrick, Miss Goodwin, Miss Kennedy, Sr Brianán and Sr Mairéad.

Marguerite James said to me of her time in secondary school: 'Playing basketball in St Louis was a great opportunity to play a team sport and many people like myself went on to play for St Louis Meteors. This club was formed in 1976 and we had many successful results in the National Premier Division. More importantly, we were able to stay connected with our school pals while developing our basketball skills.'

In this piece I would also like to acknowledge the life skills and leadership attributes that result from playing and supporting basketball at school level. Research carried out on the benefits of team sports indicate a shared sense of responsibility, a focus on others and on safety and a strong sense of civic duty. Sport helps to develop a rounded individual and contributes to positive mental and physical health. Sport also develops leadership skills and 'followership' attributes, both useful sets of skills in many areas of life. The past pupils of St Louis High School have a strong sense of being alumnae and participation in sport contributes to this sense of belonging.

I take this opportunity to wish St Louis High School continued success in both the academic and sporting arenas.

Above: St Louis cadet basketball team, winners of Division 1 League, 2013-14. Front row, from left: Claudia Alonso, Clodagh Talbot, Abbie Kearns, Cora Keegan, Nicole Landy, Amy Byrne, Saoirse Ryan and Aebrienne Cortado. Back row, from left: Amie Tunnah, Martha Malone, Grace Halton, Rebeka Lubnicka and Shannon Byrne.

Below: St Louis senior basketball team, winners of Division 2 League 2013-14. Front row, from left: Hannah Hegarty, Ingrid Awatte, Laura Granet, Eleanor Bourke, Dephyne Muzaya, Ranjeet Hasan, Patrice Benegrado and Monikarita Tolentinio. Back row, from left: Rachel Farrelly, Saoirse Nisbett, Shannon Munusami, Kate Hegarty, Lucy Butler and Sophie Shaw. Photos © Robert Allen Photography.

Vincent Kennedy

OBITUARIES

Vincent Kennedy conveys something of the contribution made by two key figures in the life of St Louis High School.

FRED WALL

Fred Wall (Freddie) came to the school in the late 1970s and was with us for about twenty-five years. He left us after a short illness on midwinter's day, 2002.

Generations of teaching and ancillary staff, not to mention countless students of St Louis High School, will remember him with affection as a gracious and quiet presence, deeply loved by anyone who engaged with him and got to know him well. He was a wonderful role model of male behaviour to innumerable impressionable teenage ladies over the years. Always calm and considerate, yet commanding great respect, he was dutiful and obliging to a fault.

He loved working in the school. People will remember him being in school from early morning and often until late at night rendering loyal and efficient service. His trademark window pole was frequently carried the length and breadth of the school like a ceremonial mace. Visitors to the school, delivery personnel and service people always asked almost in awe and anticipation for 'Mr Wall'. The Sisters in the convent also remember his great willingness to help out when asked, especially in emergencies.

Freddie was well known for his abiding interest in horse racing and Liverpool FC. The tabloid newspaper in his office remained permanently open at the sports pages!

Freddie rarely complained and if he was critical, he couched his concerns in inoffensive terms, always remaining considerate and non-judgemental. He was a bright and intelligent person and his comments and quotations, interspersed with subtle wit and irony on occasion, would often leave you smiling knowingly to yourself. He was diligent, attentive, undemanding, thorough and totally dedicated. Freddie always sought advice about tricky situations and people. He didn't ever want to impose or offend or appear uncooperative or ungrateful to anybody. To have known and worked with Freddie was an inestimable privilege. Carve his name with pride!

He displayed exemplary resignation and equanimity in the face of the tragedy of his final illness. He was greatly helped in his final weeks by the total support of his family, friends and the whole school community in Rathmines. If there are parallel universes out there, as some scientists believe, Freddie is in one marked 'Heaven'.

Fred Wall.

BRIAN Ó DUBHGHAILL

Brian Ó Dubhghaill, director of Cantairí Óga Átha Cliath, passed away on 17 October 2013. His was a very familiar and friendly face around St Louis High School for many years. Scores of pupils who joined the choir will very fondly remember this gentle, warm and considerate man, who became like a second father to them.

Brian was a consummate professional musician who took the choirs to innumerable festivals and guided them through a series of great successes, both national and international. He was hugely respected and emulated in musical circles because of his total commitment and passionate attention to detail in his work. Yet he never lost the common touch, with his gentle urging to do better, the little joke to ease a tricky exchange, the hearty laugh to break the tension and the winning smile that won him countless and devoted friends everywhere. Surely choirs of angels will accompany him on his journey to eternal rest.

Evelyn Madigan

REMEMBERING CATHLEEN NEILL

Evelyn Madigan pays tribute to a gifted and committed teacher and a supportive friend and colleague.

Many of you reading this centenary book will remember Mrs Neill as a great teacher of business subjects and a devoted year head who gave generously of her many talents during her thirty-two years of service to St Louis High School. But I remember her as a great colleague and friend.

I first met Cathleen in September 1974, as a new member of staff. She had arrived just the year previously, along with Helen Maguire, Sr Helen Power and Ann Taylor. After a stimulating staff meeting with our then principal, Sr Kathleen O'Sullivan, Cathleen shared her lunch with me – Campbell's mushroom soup. I remember it as if it were yesterday! She could see that I was finding my first day challenging as I was very shy and feeling a little overwhelmed. Cathleen's kindness to me that day was typical of her. Until her untimely death she was noted for her kindness and concern for all who crossed her path. When she died in April 2005, the huge outpouring of grief in St Louis was testament to her great contribution to the school.

First of all she was a wonderful teacher. She always got the very best out of all her students and they in their turn respected and loved her. She was one of the most understanding teachers in the school when it came to pastoral care. Students could confide in her or seek advice and were never disappointed by her response. Cathleen took part in every aspect of school life, from her duties as class teacher and year head to being on staff committees, including the staff council, going on school trips, collecting money, making tea, playing on the staff rounders team on sports day, looking after sick students, mentoring Higher Diploma students – the list is almost endless.

We started out as colleagues but Cathleen and I became very close friends. Many staff members, both teaching and non-teaching, counted Cathleen a friend. She was as generous with fellow staff members who needed a friendly ear as she was in giving her time to students. She came from a very close family whom she loved dearly and she brought all her energy, love and

loyalty to her new family when she married Ronan. Together they had three children: Stephen, Katherine and Richard. Sadly, she missed the birth of her first grandchild, born to Stephen and Claudia on the seventh anniversary of her death.

Writing about her now in the St Louis centenary year, it is sad for me to think how much she would have enjoyed not just being here for it but being actively involved. But it is a good time to remember Cathleen, the role she played in the school and all the lives she touched.

Cathleen Neill.

Ita Daly

A PEACH BY ANY OTHER NAME

*Ita Daly remembers Sr Frances Mary, aka 'Peach', principal when
she was both student and teacher in St Louis.*

Once upon a time an acquaintance of Sr Frances Teresa expressed surprise that she could cook. Her reply was, 'Well, I can read.' This, in many ways, sums up the woman I remember.

Sr Frances Teresa, aka 'Peach', was principal in Rathmines when I arrived in 1956 and was still there in 1967 when I returned to the school as a student teacher. Altogether she was principal for nineteen years, from 1951 until August 1970.

Where the sobriquet 'Peach' came from I'm not too sure, although who wouldn't be pleased to be likened to that luscious fruit? A friend, who claims that her year conferred the nickname, says that it was because of a rosy flush to the cheeks; another friend says it must have had some connection with the fact that the principal in St Mary's was known as 'Pear' (Père).

I am not convinced by either of these stories. All that wordplay seems much too sophisticated for schoolboys and girls and, as for those rosy cheeks, the Peach I remember was deathly pale, with parchment-like skin and a slightly pained expression. Her voice was low, the accent Monaghan, and I never remember her raising her voice.

She was understated, gliding through the corridors as nuns were wont to glide, taking assembly every day, popping up in unexpected

136

*At the presentation of the B&I trophy for international games in 1972,
from left: athlete Ronnie Delaney, Sr Frances Teresa, Sr Brianán,
basketball coach Don McKenna and Mr Byrne.*

places to ask you what you were doing out of class or why you weren't wearing your hat – this would be when you were on the way home and you thought it was safe to have whipped it off.

She taught English at senior level and though she wasn't an inspiring teacher, like Sr Miriam, she was fair. She had no favourites and eyed us all with a measure of dispassion – the same manner in which she eyed the world. I think she saw life as comedy rather than tragedy. The year I went back to do my Higher Diploma, Sr Frances Teresa gave me almost a full timetable.

She had more confidence in me than I had in myself but of course she knew that, despite any obvious shortcomings, I was a St Louis girl.

Once installed, I was hardly conscious of her as a principal. There may have been the odd staff meeting but they didn't loom large. She ran the school smoothly and efficiently and almost invisibly. If there were crises – and I'm sure there must have been – she handled them discreetly. She expected you to get on with your job and she left you alone to do it.

Then one day I was summoned to her office. Someone had told her (who? who?) that I was a member of the Workers' Party (Marxist-Leninist). She took my hand, as she used to when I was a difficult schoolgirl. My politics were my own business, she said, but I must be careful to keep them to myself when I was standing in front of a class.

I think what surprised me about her reaction was the lack of fuss. She was the elderly (to my eyes) principal of a convent school but she didn't seem either surprised or shocked by my political allegiance. You couldn't put Peach in a box.

She never sought popularity and I imagine that such a concept didn't even enter into her world, which was one of certainty and moral clarity. But along with that moral clarity came an understanding of human nature and her own natural kindliness.

Sr Frances Teresa was, in many ways, an old-style nun and Kathleen O'Sullivan ushered in the world of modernity when she replaced her. Yet Peach had seen it all and heard it all and taken it all in her stride. I know that generations of schoolgirls and their parents confided in her and found her, as I had, unshockable.

Anne Murray SSL

A REFLECTION ON THE ETHOS OF ST LOUIS

Former principal Anne Murray reflects on the educational philosophy of L'Abbé Louis Bautain, who founded the St Louis Institute in Juilly, near Paris, in 1842.

It is almost two hundred years since the founding fathers and mothers of the St Louis family began their work in Strasbourg. What can a twenty-first century school have in common with those early St Louis schools?

Louis Bautain, the founder of the St Louis Institute, learned his philosophy of education from Madeleine Louise Humann, the spiritual mother of the founding family. Madeleine Louise began her teaching career in the family. She was the eldest of thirteen children, and was always the 'big sister'. She was only twenty-three years old when the French revolution broke out, and within two years life in France and in Strasbourg had become very different. Catholic schools had closed and Madeleine Louise had taken on the role of teacher to her young brothers. It is no surprise that her school in Mainz and later the school in Strasbourg were notable for their strong 'family spirit'. What did they mean by that? Louis Bautain's vision of the human person is striking for those of us who may perhaps think that the insights of modern psychology have led us for the first time to cherish the individual child:

'Give the young under your protection all your care and affection and try to touch their hearts by the interest you show in them. Keep them

*Above: Monica Boyle (née Murphy) who was born in July 1914
and attended St Louis High School 1927-30, with her daughter,
Eileen (Paterson), who attended the school 1964-69.
Monica is the school's oldest surviving pupil.*

as it were under the shadow of your wings, but never force them. Respect their freedom so they will be able to choose for themselves.'

The first members of the St Louis family were formed in the tradition of the Rhineland mystics. It is not surprising, then, that they believed, like Mechtilde of Magdeburg:

> You are the sun of my life, O God,
> I am your reflection.
> When you shine, I do what I was made to do.
> I reflect God.

St Louis High School Rathmines is committed to being 'a dynamic centre of learning where all are happy and secure', a place where every member of the school community can do what she/he 'was made to do'. What struck me most about the school when I arrived there in 1980 was that it was a happy school. The second thing that struck me was the dynamic, energetic approach to education. It was my first experience of a Dublin school and I was amazed and delighted to discover that educational resources outside the school walls were so accessible and so much part of the life of the school. It was, and I know continues to be, a very creative learning environment. This is very much in the spirit of the advice given by Louis Bautain in 1837:

'Give an education that is at once solid and wide in scope, enabling the pupils to see as one whole all that concerns humankind, all the different areas of the world and all the wonders of the natural world…educated in this way, the students will be led to an understanding of the heart of things…'

So what does the 21st-century St Louis High School in Rathmines have in common with the first St Louis schools? In my opinion, all that is best of the spirit of the early schools lives on. Louis Bautain could not have begun to imagine what an education that is 'wide in scope' might mean in 2013 but I think he would be grateful to Providence that the shared 'journey towards deeper understanding in this complex world' goes on.

Brídín Gilroy

ANN RIORDAN: WHAT A LIFE!

Ann Riordan, née Kelly, the businesswoman who established Microsoft in Ireland,
is a past pupil of St Louis High School.

Ann Kelly, the eldest of a family of seven, attended St Louis Rathmines in the early 1960s. She was particularly good at maths and science but lacked confidence in language subjects. With hindsight, she feels she might have been mildly dyslexic, a condition which would, at that time, have gone undiagnosed. Believing that further academic study would be of little benefit to her, she left school after her Intermediate Certificate and was employed as a clerk in the Alliance and Dublin Consumers' Gas Company. Her abilities did not go unnoticed and, after completing her Leaving Certificate at night in Rathmines College of Commerce, she was taken from behind the desk to study Home Economics in what is now the Dublin College of Catering, Cathal Brugha Street. This led to her promotion to the position of cookery demonstrator with the Gas Company, a prestigious and glamorous job at that time. From there she went on to become a central heating designer in the then new central heating department of the Gas Company.

Ann married in 1970, the era of the 'marriage ban', whereby married women could not continue in employment in the public service, so she had to leave her job. If she hadn't had to assume the role of family breadwinner because of her husband's illness, she would have become a stay-at-home wife and mother, like so many women of her generation. Her options were stark – either she had to depend on social welfare or emigrate to a place where she would find employment to support her family. She chose the latter option and moved her family to London. Her daughter Lisa was then two and her son John six weeks old. The IT industry was in its infancy when Ann found employment with Wordplex Information Systems, a word-processing company. In a fast-changing business world driven by the rapid development of computers, Ann found her métier and after some years she was given the opportunity to return to Dublin as managing director of Wordplex Ireland.

In 1990, she was approached by Microsoft to set up Microsoft Ireland, which would promote the possibilities of the computer, then little appreciated by the general public, for both personal and commercial purposes. She was at the cutting edge of that industry through a decade of change, which saw the introduction of online banking and online shopping, activities that we now take for granted and can engage in on our phones! It was a world unimaginable when Ann started her career. She recounts how, at Microsoft Ireland in the 1990s, she received a phone call from the office of Bill Gates to ask if the founder of Microsoft could help her in promoting the company's products. She 'had to travel the highways and byways' in search of an audience to fill a room in the Shelbourne Hotel to listen to that great innovator!

Ann Riordan achieved her goal of retiring at the age of fifty – but not to stay at home. In the wake of the Good Friday Agreement of 1998 she was appointed vice-chair of Tourism Ireland. Thereafter she became a director of MIT Media Lab Europe, set up to research the use of technology in day-to-day life in the age of information. Other appointments included chair of the National Standards Authority of Ireland, Public Interest Director of the EBS, chair of Dublin Tourism, President of the Institute of Directors and board member of the Smurfit Business School. She is currently chair of the Science Foundation of Ireland, a government agency with a remit to build and strengthen scientific and engineering research and infrastructure in the areas of greatest value to Ireland's long-term competitiveness and development.

Ann attributes to her St Louis education her conviction that women can attain whatever goals they set for themselves in life – to which her exciting and fulfilling career in the upper echelons of the business world, coupled with her roles as mother and grandmother, bear eloquent witness.

PRINCIPALS OF ST LOUIS HIGH SCHOOL 1912-2014

Sr M. Raphael Nugent	1913-21	Sr Eilís Ní Thiarnaigh	1976-80
Sr M. Francisca McGowan	1921-34	Sr Anne Murray	1980-84
Sr M. Columbanus Greene	1934-36	Vincent Kennedy	1984-85
Sr M. Dympna McNama	1936-40	Sr Anne Murray	1985-86
Sr M. Ignatius Keegan	1940-45	Sr Eithne Woulfe	1986-2000
Sr Meliosa Broughton	1945-51	Eilís Humphreys	2000-05
Sr Frances Teresa McKenna	1951-70	Mary Morgan	2005-14
Sr Kathleen O'Sullivan	1970-76		

Above: Conductors of the centenary concert in Rathmines church. From left: Gráinne Gormley (past pupil), Clíona McDonough (current music teacher, St Louis High School), Rita Harrold (past pupil); Sr Pauline Johnson and Anne Purcell (past pupil).

Below: St Louis High School Instrumental Ensemble. Front row, from left: Ella Scally, Laura Conway. Middle row: Éinín Tynan, Laura Murphy, Mathilde Lyons, Meadhbh Ryan. Back row: Alice Quigley (hidden), Michaela Roche, Caoimhe Bermingham, Dervla McCormack.

Pauline Johnson SSL

ST LOUIS CENTENARY CONCERT

Pauline Johnson, former choral director of St Louis High School, describes
the celebratory centenary concert in Rathmines Church

The opening line of our St Louis hymn 'grateful notes to heaven ascending' mirrors the mind of Vivaldi, whose 'Gloria' resounded to applause in Rathmines Church on 12 December 2013. It was the perfect choice to celebrate one hundred years of St Louis High School.

Under the baton of Clíona McDonough, past pupils, teachers and parents formed a choir of eighty voices. With a chamber orchestra it gave a most professional performance that won a standing ovation. The beautiful harmonies extended far beyond the music, as past students, teachers and friends reunited joyfully in a packed church, forming another type of 'chorale' called 'the gathering', which lasted well into the morning on invitation from Mary Morgan, the school principal, to a festive supper back at the school.

Congratulations to all participants and, of course, to Clíona, for a most enjoyable evening. A nice gesture on her part was to engage a few past students (now acclaimed choral directors) to conduct the Christmas carols. Those Sisters of St Louis who instilled a great love of music in our students down the years must surely have welcomed these 'grateful notes', some now from their heavenly home.

'Gloria in excelsis Deo.'

Mary Morgan

RAISING OF THE CENTENARY FLAG

On 13 September 2013 Mary Morgan, principal of St Louis High School,
looked back on a hundred years of achievement and the
fostering of the spirit of unity in the school.

Today we mark the opening of St Louis High School, which took place on 1 September 1913, with the raising of our centenary flag. On that date a hundred years ago, the school opened in Charleville House, which is the current convent building beside us. Five Sisters of St Louis and two lay teachers were present. Thirty-six children (girls and boys) of various ages were in attendance and by 9 September 1913 that number had increased to eighty.

From the beginning the Sisters set high standards. You will notice from the prospectus that emanates from the early years that the school was described as a 'high-class secondary day school'. The curriculum was broad and included religious instruction, Irish, English, Latin, French, German, Italian, mathematics, practical and experimental science, instrumental music, singing, elocution, drawing, painting and dancing. The first aim of the Sisters was to give their pupils a sound religious training but their deportment and manners were also carefully attended to and no efforts were spared to help them acquire habits of self-control, order and neatness.

As pupil numbers increased, the Sisters gave over additional rooms in the convent, their own living accommodation, for use by the school. By 1921 there were two hundred and one pupils,

Pictured in front of the St Louis High School Centenary Timeline, from left: former principals Eithne Woulfe SSL and Anne Murray SSL and Mary Morgan, current principal of St Louis High School.

At the centenary celebrations, from left: Maura Mooney, Chair of St Louis High School Board of Management, Hannah Osuntola (deputy head girl), Eithne Woulfe SSL and Frances Martin (head girl).

and inspectors who called were 'delighted with the spirit they found in the school'. They were also 'delighted with the standard of Irish conversation'. At Christmas 1922, the play *Íosagán* was produced, along with the operetta *The Doll's Wedding*. The lighting and scenery were said to be very effective and many parents came to help, with fathers offering their services as ushers. In the early days drill displays took place annually and the most popular games were hockey and camogie.

The school expanded in various stages, first with the building of what was called St Louis Hall in 1929, followed some years later by the purchase of two houses on Grosvenor Road. Classes took place in these houses. As the numbers increased further, Assumpta Hall was built, which is now our lovely concert hall. This was a wonderful facility for the school and from 1951 onwards the high school pupils produced an opera most years. By this time, too, debating and public speaking were very important extracurricular activities with teams winning the Aer Lingus and Muintir na Tíre debates. The annals indicate that there were firsts in many competitions and high standards were much acclaimed.

In 1965 the convent chapel, now known as Cuisle, was opened. By this time there was a desire for additional sports – and so began the golden years of basketball in St Louis. Such was the enthusiasm that teams were formed in every class, resulting in success in numerous national competitions.

With the advent of free education in 1967 it was inevitable that more classrooms would be necessary and eventually, in 1982, this red brick building beside us, known as the 'new building', was opened. During all these years, the Sisters invested much of their finances in the school building, as well as giving a lifetime of dedicated service to the education of girls in the Rathmines and surrounding areas. We are indebted to them and to all former staff for their work and for the rich traditions we have inherited – traditions of music, sport, drama, debating, social awareness, inclusivity, curriculum innovation and high academic standards. We are also indebted to them for the family spirit they have fostered in our motto *Ut Sint Unum*, 'That they may be one', and, of course, our Catholic ethos.

The five Sisters who opened the school on 1 September 1913 were given a five-year probationary period by the Archbishop of Dublin, Dr Walsh, because they were regarded as being 'too progressive'! As Ms. Newman and her team of students have shown in the short video they made on the history of the school, five years have stretched to one hundred and the hundred years have yielded a rich harvest of innovation and an all-round excellent education for the girls of Rathmines and the surrounding areas. We are delighted today to be the beneficiaries of that rich harvest and though the Sisters are no longer available to teach in the school, the traditions have lived on into the new century through our membership of the Le Chéile Schools Trust, which supports us in promoting our heritage and ethos.

I am delighted that we are raising our centenary flag today and that so many former staff members who have contributed so much to our heritage are with us. In the words of Shannon L. Alder: 'Carve your names on hearts, not tombstones. A legacy is etched into the minds of others and the stories they share about you.'

Go raibh maith agaibh.

TIMELINE

The information contained in this section is based on St Louis High School over a Hundred Years, *a visual timeline devised by Evelyn Madigan, Ann Taylor and Siobhan McCanny as part of the school's centenary celebrations.*

1913
Dublin Lockout.
Rathmines Library opened.
Rathgar and Rathmines Musical Society established.
Sr M. Antonia Farrell comes from Monaghan to found the first convent in Rathmines in Charleville House.
Sr M. Raphael Nugent is first principal of the secondary school (principal 1913-21).

1914
Outbreak of First World War.
Early involvement of students in music examinations.

1916
Easter Rising.
Local pacifist Francis Sheehy-Skeffington killed in Cathal Brugha Barracks.
First St Louis dramatic production, *Which Queen, Which Faith?* staged by the Intermediate classes.

1918
End of First World War.

1919
Death of Sr M. Gabriel, one of the founding Sisters.

1920
Rathmines church closed as the result of a serious fire.

1921
Sr M. Francisca McGowan becomes principal (principal 1921-34).
Electric light comes to St Louis convent.

1922
Irish Free State (Saorstát Éireann) established
First choir examinations.
St Louis has a Feis Ceoil winner.
Plays and operettas are performed in the gym.

1924
St Louis Hall opened (September).
Vocal trio wins first prize in Feis Ceoil.

1925
President W.T. Cosgrave visits the convent.
St Louis becomes an all-Irish (A) school.

Camogie replaces hockey in the school.

1929

Senior school extended to 8 Grosvenor Road (Sacred Heart House).

1932

St Louis choir participates in Eucharistic Congress Mass in Phoenix Park.

1933

Missa Cantata is performed in the gym for the opening of the school year (the gym later becomes a chapel, later again a science lab).

1934

Opening of Rathmines Post Office.
Sr M. Columbanus Greene becomes principal (principal 1934-6.)
St Louis wins prizes for drama and dancing at Dublin Feis.
First school magazine appears.

1935

Founding of Clann Lughaidh music and drama society.

1936

Sr M. Dympna McNama becomes principal (principal 1936-40.)

1938

Students from senior school broadcast for twenty minutes on Radio Éireann.

1939

Outbreak of Second World War.
St Louis Sisters open national school in William's Park.
St Louis choir wins first prize and the cup in the Feis Ceoil.

1940

Sr M. Ignatius Keegan becomes principal (principal 1940-45).

1942

St Louis Sisters buy 7 Grosvenor Road (Wakefield House) to provide extra classroom space.
Gym converted into a chapel.

1945

End of Second World War.
Sr Meliosa Broughton becomes principal (principal 1945-51).

1948

Building fund begun for new school (concert hall block).

1949

Éire becomes the Republic of Ireland.

1950

Archbishop McQuaid formally opens the new block, comprising a concert hall and classrooms.

1951

Sr M. Frances Teresa McKenna becomes principal (principal 1951-70).
Camogie is discontinued and replaced by basketball.
The 'opera era' begins in the new concert hall.

1954

Establishment of past pupils' union.

1959

The pond is drained and tennis and basketball courts are built.

1960

Closure of Princess Cinema ('Prinner'), Rathmines.
Proinsias Ó Ceallaigh establishes Cantairí Óga Átha Cliath (Young Dublin Singers).

1965

New convent chapel consecrated.
St Louis wins Muintir na Tíre debate competition and best speaker award.

1966

Opening of new gym with six classrooms overhead.

1967

Donogh O'Malley introduces free secondary education. St Louis High School joins free education scheme.

1968

Two prefabs erected to accommodate increased student numbers.

Major basketball success (FISEC trophy) in Rome.

1969

Introduction of five-day week and parent-teacher meetings.

1970

Sr Kathleen O'Sullivan appointed principal (principal 1970-76).

Establishment of student council.

Feis Ceoil silver trophy for plainchant (for three successive wins).

1973

Ireland joins the EEC.

Students first participate in Young Scientist Competition.

1975

School joins transition year pilot scheme.

First French exchange.

1976

Sr Eilís Ní Thiarnaigh becomes principal (principal 1976-80).

Brian Ó Dubhghaill becomes director of Cantairí Óga Átha Cliath.

Earliest mention of drama festival in school magazine.

First inter-class choral festival.

1977

First school magazine (1976-77) printed outside the school.

1978

First careers seminar for 6th years.

1979

Visit of Pope John Paul II to Ireland.

1980

Sr Anne Murray becomes principal (principal 1980-86).

School library formed.

First mock interviews for 6th years.

1981

First mock election.

Phasing out of junior school begins.

1982

St Louis staff begins process of planning for 'ideal future', culminating in many initiatives involving the whole school community.

Official opening of new school building.

1983

Swan Shopping Centre (named after Swan river) opens in Rathmines.

School trip to west and east Berlin.

1984

Vincent Kennedy becomes acting principal (1984-85).

First staff council.

1985

First open day.

1986

Sr Eithne Woulfe becomes principal (principal 1986-2000).

1987

First board of management established.

1988

Dublin celebrates its millennium.

1989

Fall of Berlin Wall.

1990

Mary Robinson inaugurated first female President of Ireland. (She was also the winner in the school's mock presidential election.)

1991

First German student exchange to Bavaria.

Swimming team wins perpetual cup in Dublin Corporation gala (for fourth successive win).

Dublin named European City of Culture.

1992

First multilateral schools partnership (Comenius Project), involving schools in France and Spain.

First collaboration with De La Salle, Churchtown, in the annual drama production.

1993

First ski trip (to Austria).

Special choir established.

1994

IRA ceasefire in Northern Ireland.

1995

Seamus Heaney wins Nobel Prize for Literature.

1997

Famine commemoration mural, *Wave of Emigration*, created on outer wall of the school

1998

Leaving Certificate Applied and Vocational programmes introduced.

2000

Eilís Humphreys becomes first lay principal of St Louis High School.

Millennium concerts by choirs and orchestras from St Louis and Hunterhouse College in St Anne's Church, Dawson Street, and Belfast.

First TY participation in law course and mock trial.

First Christmas variety show.

2001

Multicultural day represents twenty nationalities from four continents from among the student body.

European year of languages.

2002

Official opening of Cuisle.

2003

Iraq War begins.

2004

Mary McAleese visits the school.

Closure of Stella Cinema, Rathmines.

2005

Mary Morgan appointed acting principal.

Tsunami in Southeast Asia.

2006

St Louis choirs from Carrickmacross and Rathmines perform Handel's *Messiah* in the Church of the Three Patrons, Rathgar.

2009

Le Chéile assumes trusteeship of St Louis High School.

School wins green flag.

Celebration of one hundred and fifty years of the St Louis Institute in Ireland.

Establishment of staff choir.

2013

Centenary celebrations.

School chosen to contribute sections for SIPTU *Lockout Tapestry*.

CONTRIBUTORS

Ella ADLER is a final year Law with History student in UCD. She has been a member of many orchestras including the National Youth Orchestra of Ireland and holds a performance diploma in violin.

Mary BLACK is one of Ireland's leading singers and is known throughout the world. Many of her albums have gone platinum and she twice sold out the Royal Albert Hall in London. She comes from a musical family and her sister, Frances, is also a well-known singer.

Angela BOURKE lectured in Irish at UCD for many years and continues to write. Her books include *The Burning of Bridget Cleary: A True Story* and *Maeve Brennan: Homesick at* The New Yorker.

Sibéal CAROLAN is a lecturer in the Institute of Leadership, Royal College of Surgeons in Ireland.

Pádraigín CLANCY facilitates retreats, pilgrimages and guided tours on Celtic heritage and spirituality in Ireland and abroad. An author, speaker, musician and dancer, she divides her time between Dublin and the Aran islands.

Máire COSGROVE taught science and maths in St Louis High School 1968-2008.

Ita DALY is a novelist and short story writer. Before that she taught for ten years in St Louis High School.

Iseult DEANE is a fifth-year student in St Louis High School.

Anne ENRIGHT is a novelist, essayist and writer of short stories. Widely translated, her books have won various awards including, in 2007, the Man Booker Prize.

Julie-Anne FINAN works as a chef in Dublin city centre and is currently in her final year of a culinary entrepreneurship degree in DIT.

Mary FINAN spent her career in public relations and is now an independent director of a number of international financial services companies.

Barbara FLEMING is now retired. Before that she was vice-principal in St Paul's, Walkinstown.

Betty FOLEY is a former English and French teacher and guidance counsellor (St Louis High School, 1972-2006).

Brídín GILROY taught Spanish, French and English in St Louis High School 1968-95 and was responsible for the promotion of the arts in the school. She was then seconded to Léargas as manager of EU education programmes in Irish primary and secondary schools and went on to serve as national coordinator of the Post-Primary Languages Initiative until her retirement in 2009.

Gráinne GORMLEY holds degrees in music, choral conducting and psychotherapy. She has been a teacher and conductor in the US and Ireland and currently works as a psychotherapist in private practice and as the conductor of the choir of St Teresa's, Clarendon Street.

Fiana GRIFFIN lectures on Irish culture and intercultural studies. Her particular area of interest is Irish stained glass in the first half of the twentieth century.

Kate HEARNE is a Baroque cellist and professional recorder player. She lives in Sweden with her husband and spends many weeks of the year on tour giving concerts with various Baroque ensembles throughout Europe.

Ursula HOUGH (Gormley) is a professional violinist who has worked in every genre of the orchestral repertoire. She currently devotes her time to serving on boards of various organisations involved in furthering music education and performance.

Yvonne JERROLD was educated at Clare College, Cambridge, and worked as an architect. As well as painting and writing poetry, she has published two novels and recently took up stone carving.

Pauline JOHNSON is a St Louis Sister and former choral director of St Louis High School.

Vincent KENNEDY is a retired deputy principal of St Louis High School.

Catherine LOANE trained as a ballet dancer and then as a pilot. She is now a captain with Aer Lingus Regional and has written a children's book, *The Eyekeeper of Ginza*.

Sadhbh McCORMACK is a jewellery designer currently working in central London. Her mother, Jane Proctor, is an artist currently working from her studio in Dublin.

Paula McNAMEE has worked in St Louis High School since the early 1990s. She teaches PE and geography and has organised many outdoor education and ski trips.

Ann-Marie MADIGAN is an astrophysicist working on stellar dynamics in Berkeley, California.

Evelyn MADIGAN was a maths teacher in St Louis High School 1974-2005.

Mary MORGAN, who was educated by the St Louis Sisters in Kiltimagh, is principal of St Louis High School.

Sharon MULDOON is a teacher of English, History and CSPE. She came to St Louis High School as a Higher Diploma student in 1990, started teaching full-time there in 1994 and continues to work happily in the school to this present date.

Anne MURRAY is a St Louis Sister. A former principal of St Louis High School, she continues to be involved in what Louis Bautain called the 'beautiful enterprise' of education, as well as in administration in the Irish region of the Sisters of St Louis.

Mary NEWMAN teachers English and is transition year coordinator in St Louis High School, where she has worked since 1993. She is very happy to be on the centenary committee.

Eilís Ní THIARNAIGH is a Saint Louis Sister who was principal of St Louis High School 1976-80. She is a historian and theologian and has published several books.

Betty Ann NORTON is director of a theatre school that celebrates its fifty-fifth birthday in 2014. She is an adjudicator, examiner and director and she writes plays.

Nessa O'MAHONY is a freelance writer and teacher. She has published three books of poetry; a fourth collection, *Her Father's Daughter,* will be published by Salmon Poetry in 2014.

Katherine O'MALLEY is a contemporary dance artist. She is currently associate dance artist with Liz Roche Company and studying to be an Amatsu therapist.

Fionnuala PARFREY is a past pupil of St Louis High School. She has a degree in English and Film Studies from TCD and is currently pursuing research in the visual arts in Paris.

Pauline SLATTERY taught English and German in St Louis High School 1969-2006.

Siobhán SUPPLE was a language teacher in St Louis High School 1975-2002 and is grateful to her students and her colleagues for the stimulation, many trips abroad and rich memories.

Jessica TRAYNOR has an MA in Creative Writing from UCD and works as literary reader for the Abbey Theatre. She teaches poetry and playwriting courses with Big Smoke Writing Factory and her first collection of poetry will be published by Dedalus Press in 2014.

Mhúin Peggy Bean Uí CHÚILLEABHÁIN in Ardscoil San Lúghaidh (Gaeilge agus Gearmáinis) 1967-2007. Bhí sí ina leas-phríomhoide 1971-6, nuair a bhí an tSiúr Caitlín Ní Shúilleabháin ina príomhoide.